Workshop Construction

DEDICATION

This book is dedicated to my two lovely kids: Julie and James.
May they one day realise that Daddy actually lives in the house with
Mummy — and not in the shed!

Workshop Construction

Planning, design and construction for workshops up to 3m (10ft) wide

Jim Forrest
and
Peter Jennings

Special Interest Model Books

www.specialinterestmodelbooks.co.uk

Special Interest Model Books Ltd.
P.O. Box 327
Poole, Dorset
BH15 2RG
England

First published 1995
This edition published by Special Interest Model Books 2011, 2013,
2018, 2023

ISBN   978-185486-131-3

Phototypesetting by The Studio, Exeter
Printed and bound in Malta by Melita Press.

Contents

FOREWORD

The whole world over there are people who have a creative interest which is very different to their everyday occupation: a hobby. To practice that interest successfully a place to work in is highly desirable, not just for somewhere to keep the tools or hide the mess, but because it is a sanctuary and a personal space.

To achieve this the workshop must be efficient, comfortable, warm and secure. Above all it must be dedicated to the user's particular needs and completely free from outside interference. So if the user can devote the time and resources to construct a workshop to meet these requirements he will be rewarded with even greater pleasure from his hobby than before — he will be able to 'escape into his own space'.

Hobbyists are very versatile people; capable of dogged perseverance in order to acquire any new skills that may be needed in the pursuit of the chosen hobby. It follows then that if given the basic scheme, few would have any problem in constructing their own workshop.

The purpose of this book is to provide a design of an easily constructed workshop, and to make the constructor aware of the essential details which must be built in for the finished building to be a complete success.

CHAPTER 1

Introduction

Approximately twenty years ago I was in a position in which I suspect many other budding modellers find themselves; wanting to make the sort of models described in the specialist press but without a suitable place in which to work. In fact, the lack of a workshop is probably the single greatest obstruction to anyone enjoying participation in a particular hobby. It certainly was in my case.

Now I know that many hobbies also require a great number of hand and machine tools but these can all be acquired in time, however a workshop in some form is needed from day one. I was lucky in that I already had a big box full of hand and cutting tools collected while serving my engineering apprenticeship and the lack of machine tools could easily be rectified because very good quality ones could be purchased from 'our' suppliers for relatively little money. No, my problem was definitely one of 'where' and until I had resolved that particular difficulty the pursuit of my chosen hobby seemed destined to remain just a mental exercise.

I had, of course, investigated the possibility of an indoor one but I backed off very rapidly when the management got aggressive! So, with that ruled out and any thoughts of building one dismissed on

the grounds of 'I couldn't do that', I just carried on reading the magazines.

Then one day one of those things happened that was destined to change everything. I was looking in the miscellaneous sales in my local paper and noticed an old Myford lathe advertised very cheaply. Totally disregarding the workshop problem I rushed off and acquired my very own lathe. Suddenly I had an overwhelming reason to finally decide upon some sort of workshop no matter how difficult, expensive or unsuitable. I ended up by buying a cheap second-hand shed from a chap who was emigrating and made that do. Freezing and draughty in the winter and smelling of creosote in the summer — it wasn't very good but at least I was modelling in something that I could proudly refer to as 'my workshop'.

Although the shed was totally unsuitable it served its purpose for a couple of years until the time came to move house. By that time its shortcomings were so annoying that my move to the new property was made without it. No ready building existed at the new place which could be used as a basis for a workshop so I appeared to be back where I had started some years before. I say 'appeared'

1

because this time there was a significant difference: I had realised that the basic elements of the simple shed could be re-engineered to produce a very solid and sound workshop that would be easy to construct and would not cost any great amount of money.

Once the family was established in the new home and the thousand and one things that hadn't been noticed when the place was viewed were done, I set to and built my very own workshop for a surprisingly small amount of money. You don't even have that? – no matter; just build part of it and finish it later when funds permit.

So what is this cheaply and easily built but at the same time substantial workshop? The main elements are shown in Detail 1.1 and, although the design developed from the humble garden shed, it has been refined to the point where it is really more akin to the modern 'system build' house (you know one of those buildings which is delivered on the back of a lorry on Monday and is being lived in on Friday!). Every part of the design has been arranged to be as simple as possible while at the same time satisfying the basic requirements of a sound, weatherproof structure.

An essential part of the design is that everything can be built with the minimum of tools, without any specialist knowledge or extensive construction works. With the exception of the base, most of the construction could be carried out in a garage and only moved to the site when the base is ready.

The simplest design is based on a straightforward floor slab arrangement with timber stud walls put together in such a way that they form immensely strong box girders. The roof is a lightweight skin that goes over the whole thing and the finished building, while it can be made to look like one if you wish, need not look anything like the humble shed from which it originates. Built into the design are all the damp courses and vapour barriers needed for full protection from the elements and the walls, floor and roof can be fully insulated as required. Detail 1.2 shows a section of a lean-to version with cross references to the chapters in the book. Although this doesn't apply to my own workshop, the structure can be built up in such a way that it could be dismantled and moved later without destroying any part of the building's integrity. Chapter 8 deals with this variation and Chapter 6 details a base which can also be moved.

Rather than just present one design of workshop, I have tried to cover variations which are likely to be built and to give some choice in the actual form of construction to suit the builder's circumstances. You will find that there are five different base types, three roofs, details for a lean-to variant and for a typical garage conversion. So with a bit of mix-n-match you should be able to build something to your own taste, skill and pocket.

Before we delve into the construction part there are just a few points which are worth mentioning at the start:

(1) The design has been vetted by my collaborator in this book; Peter Jennings. He is a qualified Registered Architect well versed in the theory and practice of building construction. Peter also prepared the drawings which appear throughout the text.

(2) There are limits to everything and that applies to this design of building. The one dimension which controls the sizes of the structural members is the roofspan and the maximum for this design is 3m (nom

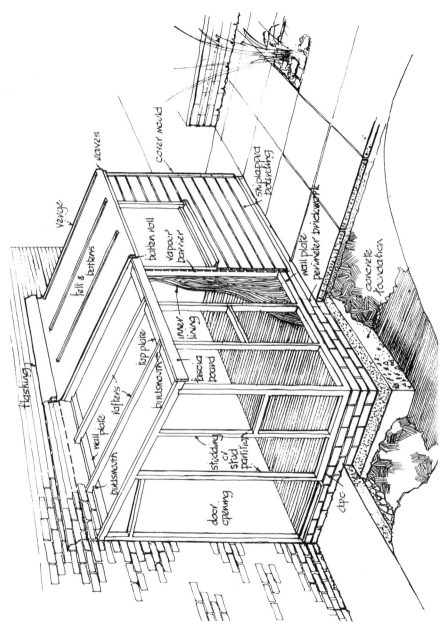

Labels on the drawing:

flashing
verge
eaves
felt & batterns
battern roll
vapour barrier
cover mould
shiplapped boarding
wall plate
perimeter brickwork
concrete foundation
rafters
wall plate
top plate
birdsmouth
inner lining
birdsmouth
fascia board
wall plate
studding or stud partition
door opening
dpc

Detail 1.1 The self-build workshop. Lean-to version showing main elements.

3

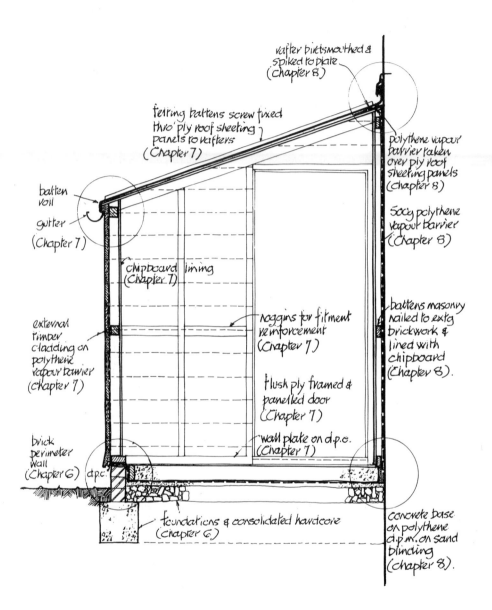

rafter birdsmouthed &
spiked to plate
(Chapter 8)

firing battens screw fixed
thro' ply roof sheeting
panels to rafters
(Chapter 7)

polythene vapour
barrier taken
over ply roof
sheeting panels
(chapter 8)

batten
voll
gutter
(Chapter 7)

chipboard lining
(Chapter 7)

500g polythene
vapour barrier
(Chapter 8)

external
timber
cladding on
polythene
vapour barrier
(Chapter 7)

noggins for fitment
reinforcement
(Chapter 7)

battens masonry
nailed to extg
brickwork &
lined with
chipboard
(Chapter 8).

flush ply framed &
panelled door
(Chapter 7)

brick
perimeter
wall
(Chapter 6)   d.p.c.

wall plate on d.p.c.
(Chapter 7)

foundations & consolidated hardcore
(Chapter 6)

concrete base
on polythene
d.p.m. on sand
blinding
(chapter 8).

Detail 1.2 *Typical section through workshop, lean-to version.*

4

10ft) – based on the assumption that most will be around 2.5m (nom 8ft). This need not be too much of a limitation because the workshop can be as long as you like.

(3) Throughout the chapters on construction there are details on the sizes of the various structural parts for a range of spans. *Do not go below the figures given because they have already been trimmed to the lowest that Peter will agree to put his name to!*

(4) My own workshop is built to this design and has shown no deterioration since the day it was finished in 1985. Two years ago I extended it by 50% during a week off from work without any problems.

(5) The upper construction is of wood and, as we all know, this often isn't seen as the best material for long term exterior use in a wet, damp climate such as in Britain. This isn't because it is an unsound building material (as our Continental and North American friends will quickly tell us); it is because we do not design for the wood to be in a wet climate so it rapidly deteriorates. Great care has been taken to cover this in the detailing and your new workshop will not rot away.

(6) It should be borne in mind that any relatively small, free-standing wood structure is bound to have some limitations as to how much abuse it can be expected to withstand. You can beef up the whole structure by simply linking it to an existing wall, but if you intend to install heavy machinery then you really need a more substantial design of building. This design has proved perfectly satisfactory for an 'average engineer's shop' with a couple of

lathes, drilling and milling machine, and the usual bench with equipment for persuading metal to go where it doesn't at the moment! It will be equally suitable for many other hobbies including carpentry, aircraft modelling, radio hams etc.

(7) Britain's building industry never really took on the true meaning of metrication and this can be seen only too well in the so-called metric dimensions which are no more than direct conversions of imperial ones. Some sheet materials, such as plasterboard, are metric but that's probably only because they are made or sold in large quantities on the Continent. However, it doesn't really matter because very often the sizes stated for wood are not the actual size as purchased anyway – they were the sizes before it was machined at the sawmill! So, because we Brits are supposed to have a full grasp of metric dimensions, and because our Continental friends will never understand feet and inches, I have decided to give all of the dimensions in metric alone except where they relate to the nominal sizes of the whole workshop when the English equivalent is also given. The Appendix has a conversion table if you need it.

(8) No-one wants to erect a building which is no more than a permanent liability and correct detailing will help guard against this. The detailing alone though can't guarantee a problem-free life; just as important is the careful selection of the most suitable materials for the job in hand. No doubt you will be able to find cheaper alternatives for the same purpose but this is not recommended as they will not be

durable enough. This may appear to be in conflict with the basis of this exercise — that of producing a good workshop at a low price — but the truth is that in certain situations some materials are just not good enough.

(9) Precision hobbyists, such as model engineers, cabinet makers and aeromodellers, do not make good builders. It's not that their construction is faulty, it's just too good! Precision workers will spend hours and hours checking such things as levels, straightness and circularity whereas builders don't. In fact builders' work is a big collection of imperfections — and the result usually looks just right! (I feel a strong temptation to say that builders don't even know what straightness, level or circularity are — especially the one that built my house — but knowing my luck it will turn out that they are prolific modellers, read this book, and come looking for me!) If you do build your own workshop try to relax about all these things because the odd 3mm here or there just doesn't matter.

(10) Read the book before even thinking about what you want, what you need or what you think you are capable of building. It is littered with ideas, alternatives, shortcuts and easily followed construction notes. Having read right through you will be in a better position to decide what type of workshop will suit your needs, pocket and building skills.

(11) Finally, there are very few photographs of the construction of my workshop included because I did not take many! At the time I had no idea that I would write this book so the photographs were not taken as purpose-built illustrations. Unfortunately, as the finished building is situated in a relatively narrow gap between the house and a wall it is difficult to take a good shot.

CHAPTER 2

Planning and design

There are two parts to the planning process. This chapter deals with the first part, which is the design, location and internal layout of the projected workshop, and Chapter 3 will cover the second part which deals with the local planners and their regulations as operated by local authorities. I would strongly suggest that you complete your own planning stage before approaching the authority as they are going to need to know details of size, location and use etc. before they will be able to advise you on your position. However, you can't just go ahead blindly with your planning – there are rules which you must adhere to. The first thing that you need to know then is the rules.

Constraining rules

The regulations for my area (Hampshire, England), are as follows and it is reasonably certain that they will be much the same in yours:

(1) Under the Town & Country Planning Act 'a permanent extension for residential purposes may be constructed and considered as Permitted Development under the Act provided that it does not exceed 10% of the volume of the building or 70 cu.m (2470 cu.

ft); whichever is the greater'. These figures relate to the *original* building size and any subsequent extensions must be taken into account when calculating the maximum volume that would be permitted. It is important to realise that any existing house extension could have a direct bearing upon the size of any additional structure that would be allowed under the Permitted Development rule. The converse of this is that the workshop could limit the size of any future extension, such as a conservatory or a garage, and could even prevent any further development on the site at all. It is worth noting that the volume includes the roof volume, so a high pitched roof might put you outside the rules.

(2) Many local authorities control the size and siting of ancillary buildings by applying a percentage ratio to the area of the building in relation to the whole plot. Thus, a large structure in a small plot may not be allowed, but a similar structure in a big plot would be suitable. It is therefore important that you keep your building in scale.

(3) You should not build in front of the house sightline. This means that your

building should not project out from the front of your house or the general frontage of a line of properties.

(4) In many cases a minimum distance of 20 metres (65ft) from a *main* highway must be maintained free of any sheds or other outbuildings.

(5) The height of outbuildings is usually restricted to single storey — around 2.4m (8ft) and this should be observed. A complication arises when pitched roofs are considered because any single-storey building with a pitched roof will clearly break the height restriction. It is generally accepted (and the rules are very vague on this point) that for the purposes of the rules, a pitched roof height should be calculated as one third of the actual vertical height. Add this dimension to your eaves height and make sure it is below 2.4m. In practice, try to keep the all-up height to 3m or less and you should be OK. Please also note that while a little shed tucked away in the depths of the property is unlikely to offend anyone, a 15m mast on the roof will not go down too well!

(6) If your site has already been developed to the point where the shed will put you outside the permitted development rule, then you must take advice from the planners. Being outside of the rule does not mean that you can't build it — you have probably just got to do a bit more paperwork.

(7) The landlord must be made aware of any development that goes on his land. So, if you rent or lease the property, make sure that you tell him.

It must be understood that this is a complex area which can be subject to a great deal of interpretation by authorities according to their own local conditions. If you have any doubts about what you might be allowed to do then contact the local planning department at the civic offices. In theory the planners are there to help and should be able to guide you with specific local regulations so that you do not find them at a later date standing on your doorstep and looking for a fight!

The aforementioned relates only to the position in the UK. If you live elsewhere then please make sure that you find out about any regulations and laws which affect your venture. Every district will have an authority or council charged with implementing and enforcing the local and national planning laws — find out where it is and who you need to talk to.

Bearing these limitations in mind, you can now move on to look in depth at the planning and detailed design of the workshop.

Siting

The most important part of your own planning procedure must be to decide where the workshop can go. If you are lucky and have a choice of situations then you can move on to the remaining details such as size and internal layout. The chances are that this will not be the case. The siting may have a significant bearing on the planning to follow by placing constraints upon you. Pick the location carefully as once it is built you won't be in any hurry to move it. The following notes are points which you may want to consider before making a final decision.

Access

An important point first: if you are an inveterate tea or coffee drinker don't build the thing right down the end of the garden or you will wish that you hadn't every time it rains!

Do remember to take into account

what the result of your activity will be — so don't make the same mistake as the chap who built a motor yacht in his backyard and then had to demolish his house extension to get it out!

Services

You will have to get electrical power out to the building at the very least and, depending on the workshop's particular purpose, you may need a water supply. The water isn't really a problem as a run of 22mm domestic water pipe will provide an adequate supply over a great distance. The power supply is a different proposition though. Every metre of cable run carries the penalty of a power drop so the rating of the cable has to go up. So, when deciding on the position take into account where you can pick up the supply from the house and whether you can run a cable either overhead or underground.

Linked structure

Think carefully before you build it onto one of the house walls because vibration and noise — especially low frequency noise — travels far better in solids than in air. You could find considerable opposition to your using the shop once it is built and a noise or vibration problem is revealed. Even worse, if you live in a semi-detached house then you could find your activities severely limited by your neighbour's kiddies' bedtime.

However, there is a lot to be said for building onto the side of an existing wall, be it a garage or a garden wall. Not only does it lead to a more rigid structure and reduce the amount and cost of construction, it also provides a solid plane to build off. A further advantage is that of weather protection in that the wall can be used to shelter the workshop from prevailing winds; very important in the

north-east of England and the flatlands of Europe.

Ground condition

If you do have a choice over the location, select the hardest ground with the most level position that you can and avoid an area where water tends to collect. Try not to use ground which is currently under cultivation as it will probably have a deep topsoil layer which will be very loose and difficult to compact. Picking a suitable site could save you a tremendous amount of work on the base later.

Security

Tucking the workshop away is probably a good idea in today's world, but don't tuck it away in some far corner of a large garden. Burglars love isolated buildings where they can take their time and not worry too much about the noise they make. If the finished building will be readily visible to casual or prying eyes then make provision for adequate screening.

Boundary lines

Try to avoid siting it very close to or on the boundary. Allow at least half a metre for maintenance of both the fence and the building. In doing so you will avoid any damage to the boundary fence, which may well be owned by your neighbour.

A further problem with building on the boundary line is that your foundations, no matter how small, may actually be on your neighbour's property — and he can insist that you remove them!

It is surprisingly easy to 'wind-up' neighbours. They are just going to love you for building a shed right in the light of their lounge window or obscuring the view of the cathedral. Legally they don't have any inherent right to light or a view — but that won't stop them from complaining to all and sundry!

Expansion

When I first built my workshop I had one small lathe, a small drilling machine and a bench grinder. At the time I thought that I had all of the machine tools I would ever need and my workshop was ample in size. 'Ample' meant that I could just squeeze in a milling machine. The end result? A crowded workshop in need of expansion! Fortunately I had sited the building in a position which allowed me to extend it relatively easily. (For those people who are now thinking that I should have stopped myself from overstuffing the original workshop space I have only one thing to say — *go and take a look in your garage!*)

If at all possible allow for future expansion because you never know what lies some years ahead. A change of hobby; a change in the scale being worked to or suddenly having to share with an up and coming son or daughter can all result in the original building being too small.

If you have a reasonable area available then you probably won't have many problems with the siting placing constraints on the size or layout of the workshop. However, it may well be that the best or most suitable location for many reasons will actually lead you to make some compromises. In my own case there was a strip of garden down the side of the house which was bounded by two garden walls and, ideal as the site for the workshop, it wasn't very wide. This led to the construction of a 2m (6ft 6in.) by 4m (13ft) long structure which I have now extended to 6m (20ft) long. A size of 3m x 4m would have been better but it would have had to be sited in a much less suitable position for other reasons.

Once you know where it is to be erected, and are aware of the restrictions on its size and shape, you can start to consider the interior layout.

Interior layout

Occasionally we are lucky enough to see inside other modellers' workshops via the pages of the specialist press. What this has shown me is that we all work differently and have vastly differing equipment layouts. This can probably be explained by the fact that most people start with an orderly layout of just a few machines and, as new ones are obtained, they are shoe-horned in with the minimum disruption to existing equipment. Try to avoid this by not building something that is barely big enough to enclose your existing equipment, or, if there will be space to spare, leave it spare rather than spreading your equipment out to fill it. On the other hand, if you are starting small for financial reasons, definitely plan the interior for expansion later.

Laying out a workshop is surprisingly difficult because it is not until you start 'making' that you begin to realise where the best positions for the various bits of kit are. Then there is the complication of equipment additions and upgrades. What surprised me is just how quickly other 'desirable' machines are obtained. In fact, it almost becomes a mission in life once the workshop is up. This is where the design of this workshop can be used to help us because it is easy to extend and accommodate future gains.

It's worth spending a lot of time on the layout because (I firmly believe) all Homo Sapiens are inherently lazy and any obvious waste of effort is seen as a fundamental fault and a cause of endless irritation thereafter. In other words, if you get the layout badly wrong it will be a constant source of annoyance for evermore. This is where time spent on planning will later prove to be time well spent. So where do you start? As good a place as any is on the basis of existing knowledge.

In about the 1950s a group of social scientists developed the very plausible theory of the Ergonomic Triangle. It was based on the relative positions of the sink, cooker and worktop, so you can guess what they were working on. Despite its 'domestic' origin the theory is very relevant to us. The top of the triangle is the point around which all operations centre: in the case of the kitchen it was the sink and in our context it will be the workbench. The other two points on the triangle will be the next most used areas in the workshop – probably the lathe and the drill in an engineer's shop and the machining centre and fretsaw in a woodworker's shop. The idea is that you should travel the minimum distance from the central element to any other element in the room. From this you can see that the ideal layout of a work area must be square with the bench on one side and the machines on the other, or oblong with at least enough width to achieve the same end. Detail 2.1 shows the basic idea.

I think that I can vouch for the validity of the theory because for the reasons stated earlier, my workshop doesn't conform and it's a confounded nuisance. My bench is right up one end, the lathes are halfway down and the milling machine is right at the other end. I seem to have to walk miles to get anything done and it is amazing just how often I get to the mill only to find I've left something on the bench! (I should point out that I was aware of this fault when I built the workshop but it was one of the compromises that I had to make in order to build it in the 'best' location.)

While most of the dimensions will be decided by what you intend to do in the building and the available space, those relating to the height of the ceiling are more or less fixed. Detail 2.2 shows a section of a typical workshop with two sets of dimensions, one of which is in brackets. The unbracketed dimensions should be used if you are not restricted by height such as building against a low existing wall. The bracketed dimensions are the minimum that can used in the event of a height restriction. Think carefully before deciding upon a low roof height for any reason than absolute necessity – a low ceiling will not only spoil the 'feel' of the room but will also place restrictions on the positioning of the door.

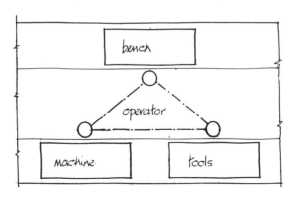

Detail 2.1 *The ergonomic triangle.*

11

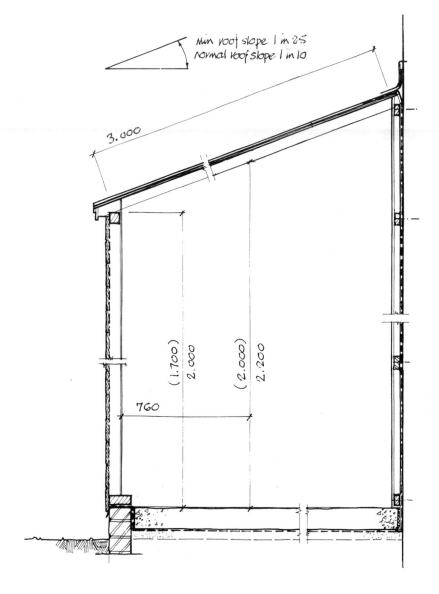

Min roof slope 1 in 25
normal roof slope 1 in 10

3.000

(1.700) 2.000

(2.000) 2.200

760

Detail 2.2 *Optimum and minimum workshop dimensions (minimum dimensions in brackets).*

If you are in a position to have full control over the size and shape then you can do as you please with the internal layout. If there are constraints on you then you will just have to try to get the best compromise that you can. You are on your own as far as the fine details of the layout are concerned because it rather depends on what you intend to do in the workshop.

While it is not possible to give specific details on the layout, there are some general points that you might like to take into consideration.

(1) Sheet timber, the basic material that we will be using for the internal wall lining, is produced in 2.4 × 1.2m sheets (the old 8ft × 4ft size). The 2.4m dimension will be cut to suit the height of the internal ceiling and, if only exact multiples of 600mm (half the width) are used on the wall lengths, then you can achieve the maximum economy of material and minimise the amount of cutting that you will have to do. Don't forget that the lengths concerned are the *internal* wall lengths.

(2) One mistake that I made when I first built my workshop was in the length of the workbench. This was corrected when I built the extension because even though I don't construct large models, I have had to increase its length from 1m to 2.5m long — 2m for tool scattering and 0.5m to work in!

(3) The position of the door can be a very important factor regarding the amount of usable space available. I would suggest that you only position it once you have an idea of the internal layout and it may be better to arrange for it to open outwards rather than inwards. That way it doesn't intrude into the workspace

when it is opened — rather important in narrow workshops — and it is easier to seal against the weather.

(4) Windows are nice to have but they can be a nuisance if you put them in the wrong place. If you like everything to hand while sitting at the bench don't put a window right in front of you because you will probably wish later that you'd put a shelf there instead. They are also the easiest way for unwanted visitors to get in so avoid big picture windows unless you are sure that they can be made secure.

(5) The subject of windows raises the question of lighting. There can be little doubt that natural light is the most effective medium to work in but it is impossible to control or predict. Placing a machine adjacent to a large window may allow you to get the best from the light available but it could also cause some problems. Windows concentrate light so it can get uncomfortably hot next to one. They also cause glare so if you position a bench or machine badly you could end up with a persistent squint. If you really get it wrong and put a window in a west-facing wall you could end up with so much light coming in around sunset that you just won't be able to look from the east end to the west end.

(6) It may pay you to take account of prevailing weather conditions. On the north-east coast of England for instance, it would not be advisable to put the door and window on the east-facing wall because of the severe weather which can come from that direction. Always try to locate any wall openings on a sheltered side.

(7) Take into account how you intend

to keep the place warm. The design provides for full insulation but it will still need a considerable amount of heat in the winter. Most heaters need a clear area around and above them so they can take up a fair amount of space. Think carefully before deciding on paraffin and bottled gas heaters. Apart from having live flames they also pump considerable amounts of moisture into the air. (Chapter 9 covers the area of heating in the workshop.)

(8) If you are starting out with a small shop but have every intention of gaining more machinery later, allow for this by leaving one end of the shop unrestricted on the outside and avoid placing almost immovable equipment at that end on the inside. Then, when you are in a position to build the extension, it will be relatively easy.

(9) If cash is really short there is no need to abandon the project or cut corners on the materials. Both are bad mistakes. It is better to build small and squeeze everything in until finances allow you to enlarge it. If you don't want to start with a very small shop just lay the base — once you've done that (and nearly got a workshop) I guarantee that the rest will follow in a very short time!

(10) The workshop can be built to allow the whole structure to be dismantled and moved to another site. I must admit that this may seem to be a daunting task to those of us who already have workshops and would probably need six months just to pack up the contents, let alone the building! In fact, anyone building a demountable workshop would also fit it out in such a way that removal of the contents would be easy. Obviously you should decide on this variation before starting to build and not halfway through. (The demountable variation is covered in Chapter 8.)

(11) In common with just about all model engineers, I am totally incapable of throwing anything away. The trouble is that after having saved something I seem to retain just a vague memory that I have it but the exact location totally escapes me every time! Storage aplenty is absolutely essential in a workshop; both in the form of open shelving and cupboards. If you can, try to allocate the space at the design stage even if you don't actually install it immediately. It might stop you from having to squeeze it all in later when perhaps it isn't so easy because of other added equipment.

(12) If you are the 'clubby' type, or know other people with the same interest, talk to them about their workshops and how they use them. Such people are a great source of information, not just on the layout, but also on machinery, suppliers etc.

There are probably a thousand and one other considerations which apply variously to certain hobbies and not others. You should already know of any that are specific to your own. Try to think of them all and take them into account. The more time spent in considering the design of the building and its layout , the greater will be the reward in its use.

Exterior design

Once you have decided on the interior layout you can think about the external design. When I say think about it I mean exactly that — because there isn't very much you can alter in the design being put forward here! All you can really do is fiddle about with the positions of the door and windows. The walls are timber clad and that amounts to strip cladding or sheet covering; not much room for variation there. The only area where there is a choice is in the type of roof. The simplest, both to construct and in cost terms, is the single slope or mono-pitch type. If you fancy something a bit more decorative you can build the conventional centre pitched type roof. The mono-pitch roof can have a surprisingly shallow slope, but a steeper slope is preferable in order to allow water to run off the roof quickly. Whatever you do, do not build a flat, or near flat, roof. Once water can lay on a rooftop it will eventually find its way through the proofing and into the building. The actual detailed design of both roof types is covered in Chapter 7, but if you intend to build a workshop with a roofspan over 2.4m (8ft) then it would be best to choose the pitched roof type because the size of rafters needed above this get so big that it becomes very expensive.

Finally, keep it simple. Entry vestibules, rooflights etc. are all very nice but they introduce the possibility of problems with the building's integrity. Simplicity has to be the keyword here.

Armed with size of the building you can now progress to working out how much it will cost (see Chapter 4 for ideas on keeping the cost down) and to getting organised for starting construction. If you have followed the official planning regulations you can also approach the local authority with a reasonable certainty of being allowed to proceed unhindered but, before you do, read the next chapter for guidance.

CHAPTER 3

Statutory regulations

With a bit of luck you now know the size and position of your workshop but, before you go mad with the spade, protect yourself against being torpedoed from below by advising the local authorities of your intentions. It doesn't guarantee future bliss but it will go a long way towards it. Whether you inform them or not is up to you – I'm sure that many don't bother without any ill effect. *Even if you decide not to you must at least know and abide by the official regulations.*

Planning permission

The following sentence appears to be a complete contradiction but is in fact correct. You will not require approval for a structure provided it complies with the regulations and is approved as such. This is because this type of structure should not require specific planning permission from your local authority providing it complies with the regulations laid down in the Town and Country Planning Act and can be categorised as 'permitted development'. All councils operate the Town and Country Planning Act and most have various local planning by-laws of their own. Providing you are aware of, and observe the guidelines and restrictions on all building work in your area, you can

erect any reasonable building for your own use.

It follows then that provided you observe the rules, in theory there is no need to tell the authority at all. The problems arise when specific local by-laws alter them or, as is the case with all rules, there is a difference in their interpretation between you and the authority.

The actual rules were included in Chapter 2 and I won't repeat them here – but if you skipped them it would pay you to read them now before continuing.

You must bear in mind that local planning law is a complex area which is subject to much interpretation (and possibly manipulation) by authorities according to their own local conditions. The only satisfactory way to be sure that your 'development' is OK is to telephone the relevant department and, if necessary, send a sketch showing the plot with existing buildings, the new one and a brief description of its construction and use. It doesn't have to be very fancy; just reasonably accurate enough to show that the rules are not being bent. The result should be a notification that it complies with the Permitted Development Rule and that you can proceed.

All sounds very easy doesn't it? The

problem is that dealing with a local authority very often isn't as straightforward as perhaps it should be. Get it wrong and you may end up wishing that you had not got up that morning! Here's a few tips to help you avoid steering a collision course with the Establishment.

(a) At all times in dealing with the authority it should be made quite clear that the building is solely for private domestic use in the pursuance of a hobby.

(b) Whatever you do avoid the word *workshop*. The uninitiated will translate it into 'metal bashing shop, factory, car repair shop etc.'. Start that ball rolling and you really *will* wish that you hadn't got up!

(c) Be very careful about upsetting the neighbours. It has been said that it's not where you live, it's who you live next to! I cannot stress the truth of that statement enough. What's more, it works both ways — would you like to live next to a bloke who seems to spend all day planing wood down for the local DIY shop?

One objector could scuttle the whole thing. This may not occur at the outset of course because the neighbour will not know about your plans (or your interest). It may well be some time after the council have given the nod and the workshop is up when this little gem hits you! If it does then you are on a loser. Gone are the days when you could do as you please in your own home. Local authorities are legally obliged to investigate every complaint received from the general public, so if you upset someone it could be really bad news. If you can, cultivate your neighbours and let them know what you do in your spare time. (Most creative hobby people are quite useful to know at times — especially if they can fix radios or make bits for a broken lawnmower.) Having done this and built your workshop you must then respect your neighbours' rights and not be a nuisance.

The obvious cause of conflict is noise but it isn't the only one by any means. Building the workshop in a position which blocks a neighbour's light or destroys a view is another. I'm sure you can think of many more.

The cost of getting this bit wrong can be very high. If you receive a visit from a council official you could find yourself standing on, very thin ice indeed. Despite protestations on your part to the effect that the workshop is just a hobby room, he may, (as a way of solving the nuisance problem), disagree and decide to categorise it as 'commercial' and therefore a 'prohibited development'. If that happens you can expect to receive an enforcement order very soon. (An enforcement order will order the demolition of said structure by a given date.)

(d) Planners are a suspicious lot and not without cause. There are people around who have erected 'garages' under the Permitted Development rule and then let them out as holiday homes! One of your primary jobs must be to ensure that the building is clearly nothing other than what you say it is. You don't need me to tell you then that it would be courting trouble to install a bay window, a fitted toilet or anything else that could give them reason to issue an enforcement order.

(e) Do not be tempted to understate your intentions. There is a big difference between a 2m × 2m potting shed and a 6m × 6m one.

(f) Do not try to make a statement with the building and finish it in the form of a Great Western Railway Station or a period piece of furniture!.

(g) Do not construct something which is clearly unsafe or ugly.

There are certain areas though where very strict local planning laws prevail — such as in conservation areas and around listed buildings. Even a simple garden shed can be a job to get built in these regions. If you live in such an area then contact your local authority before going too far because planning permission is *always* required in these situations.

It might also be worth racking your brains to remember what your solicitor said at the time that you bought the property. Did he, for instance, utter the words "restrictive covenants"? If he did then have a look at your copy of the deeds — you may find that a covenant exists which prohibits any development whatsoever. (For the record my own and adjacent properties have some restrictive covenants relating to further building. As far as I can see no-one has taken a blind bit of notice of them and, as many houses now have extensions, the council must have approved them for building regulations compliance at least.)

Building regulations (UK)

Building regulations exist to ensure that structures erected in the UK meet minimum standards regarding structural integrity, insulation levels etc. They are aimed at houses and offices etc. and do not apply at all to sheds or other minor outbuildings. Once the authorities are aware that you are constructing nothing more than a shed, they will lose interest in the venture and that will be the end of your commitment to them. You can then start building safe in the knowledge that you have complied with the rules. If you find you're getting involved in discussions about building regulations then you have gone seriously wrong somewhere.

Although you will not have to comply with the building regulations, under the Health Act you have a statutory obligation to ensure that anything you erect does not or will not constitute a hazard to others. Whatever you do, ensure that the structure is safe. If you are unsure about anything then either ask someone, or grossly oversize it.

Other regulations

We live in a world just brimming with regulations, regulators and legislators who spend their whole lives introducing even more regulations. It's a situation that seems to be out of control. Once upon a time they only applied to industry and agriculture, but not now. Now we all have to observe regulations like the Control of Substances Harmful to Health Act and the Control of Pollution Act — which is the one that carries weight on noise pollution and nuisance. Most people need not be concerned about them as commonsense makes the rules unnecessary. So, if you do use nasty substances make sure that you treat them as such and provide for their storage and disposal accordingly. The Pollution Act is the one to really worry about though. It covers noise pollution, (among many others), and can be used against you with great severity, including seizure of your equipment. (Don't get me wrong on this score, I am not opposed to applying control where control is required, but regulations can be abused and manipulated. When this happens to an industry it usually has sufficient resources to protect itself but individuals stand very little chance of a decent defence.)

CHAPTER 4

Tools and materials

Tools

No matter what work needs to be done, tools are always required; sometimes simple tools can suffice but very often some highly specialised ones are needed. Fortunately for us the construction of a simple workshop like this doesn't really require any very special tools and most people's garden shed will have all the basic tools that are needed.

You could get by with just the following ordinary tools:-

Hammer
Spade or shovel
Tape measure
Spirit level
Woodsaw
Small square
Electric drill
Mortar trowel
1.5m × 1.5m wooden board (for mixing concrete on)
Screwdrivers
A friend who owes you a favour!

There are however other tools which could save you a lot of hard work and a fair amount of head scratching. Some can easily be home-made but others need to be begged, borrowed or hired. So if your lumbars are forever telling you that they are old or, if you can no longer jerk a bag of cement up onto your head at least fifteen times, then I suggest you look in your local paper for sources of these labour savers. Look under 'services' or 'miscellaneous' as there always seems to be someone prepared to hire out this sort of kit very cheaply. Alternatively, most towns have equipment hire shops and the rates are usually very reasonable.

These are the real labour saving ones:-

Cement mixer
Electric screwdriver
Power saw
Wheelbarrow
Sack barrow
Staple gun

There are also some tools you can make yourself and so make your life even easier:

Builder's level
Deadmen (2)
Tamper
Rocking wedge
A large square

For those who are not familiar with this last list of tools, a **builder's level** is a very

19

long level (min. 900mm), and usually made of wood. You can make a reasonable facsimile by strapping a short level to a decent piece of straight timber which is parallel along its length. Alternatively you can buy a bubble (don't laugh – you really can!) and set it into a suitable length of timber with silicone mastic. Set it up on something previously checked for level with a normal short level.

Deadmen are T-shaped poles about 50mm higher than your ceiling will be and are used to hold up the ceiling panels while you try to bang the nails in. Anyone who has tried to do it without any deadmen will know exactly how useful they are! Simply screw a short length of 50 × 25 at 90 degrees to one end of another piece of 50

× 25 to form a 'T' which is just higher than your ceiling will be. Add a couple of cross braces and you are in business (see Detail 4.1). To use them, all you have to do is rest the ceiling panel on the tee end and jam it against the rafters by wedging the 'leg' against the floor. Put one at each end of the panel and then you will have two hands free to put the nails in.

A **tamper** is simply a heavy weight on the end of a pole and is used to compact the ground. Any old weight will do providing it is flat underneath – and providing you can lift it repeatedly! If you don't have a convenient weight then cast a concrete one in an old plastic bucket with a broom handle sticking out of it.

The **rocking wedge** is a strip of timber

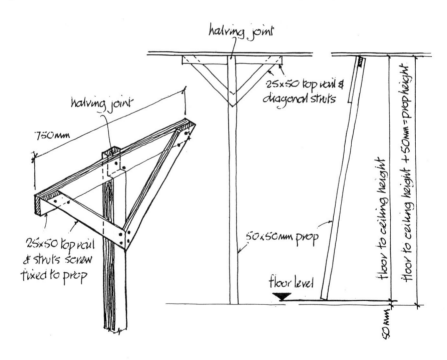

Detail 4.1 *Deadman assembly.*

20

approximately 50 × 300 × 25mm thick with a 25mm square × 50 long crosspiece fixed about 100mm from one end as a fulcrum so it forms a lop-sided seesaw (see Detail 4.2). It is used when placing the internal wall sheets to jack the panels up against the ceiling. Just rest the sheet against the wall with the short end of the wedge under it and press down with your foot on the other end – up goes the panel!

The final one is a **large square**. This is not essential because you can check for squareness by the simple expedient of measuring across the diagonals. Alternatively, you could make up a long-sided try-square from convenient bits of timber using the corner of one of the wallboards as a template. What would be really useful though is a square against which you can cramp the timber while constructing the framework so that you automatically end up with a 90 degree angle. Such a device is shown in Detail 4.3. I will not try to describe its construction because it is obvious from the sketch.

Materials

Wood

The main material of construction is wood, a material which most engineers don't have much love for. To those who don't usually use it, wood is a material which bends, shatters, splits, warps, and of course, rots. As an engineering material it is pretty diabolical, but for buildings it is ideal provided it is used properly.

Although we never think of it this way, wood is just dead trees and, in common with all natural materials, Nature has developed many ways to return it into the carbon cycle in the shortest possible time. The biggest threat is from water, followed by fungus, bacteria and then insects. The builder's job is to ensure that his structure is designed to eliminate these threats, and this is where the detailing becomes so important because it is the little details which ensure that these enemies are kept at bay.

Wood does in fact have a lot going for it:

It is an extremely good insulant
It is a good acoustic barrier
It is very easy to work
It is relatively cheap
Used correctly it can be immensely strong
It is often very decorative

No, I don't work for the Forestry Commission! Although it is relatively cheap the

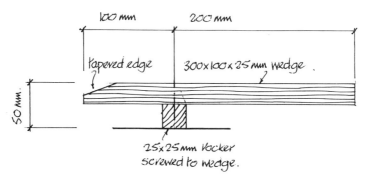

Detail 4.2 *Rocking wedge assembly.*

21

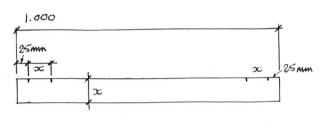

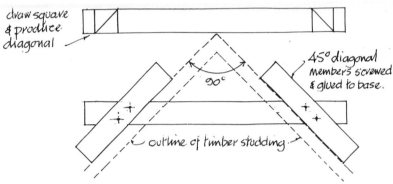

Detail 4.3 *Large square assembly.*

quality is often a bit 'iffy'. The cause is fast-grown 'regenerable stock' timber and forced air kiln drying which tries, usually without success, to mimic proper seasoning. In fact some wood twists all over the place as soon as it is exposed to the outside world and often looks as though it will take root if you stand it on damp ground! Pick your wood very carefully and don't buy it in a sealed polythene wrapping — go for the stuff that has been racked off outside as any that would twist will have done so and you can avoid it. It is not necessary to buy the expensive planed timber as rough sawn is perfectly suited for our purpose. It may however be worth paying that little bit extra for timber which has been pressure injected with preservative and insect repellent. Finally, if buy-

ing from a timber specialist, ask for the timber to be regularised — that way it should be the same size. If buying from a DIY store try to get it all from the same source at the same time because then it should all be relatively consistent in its size. That may seem a little daft — after all 50 × 50 is 50 × 50 . . . isn't it? Not in the world of wood it isn't. The 50 × 50 will be the size it started at before they pushed it through the finishing machine so it could be a lot smaller. Even unfinished, or rough sawn, timber probably still won't be 50 × 50 because all sizes are 'nominal'.

The only area where good quality timber is required is in the floor joists — if you are using a timber floor of course. For obvious reasons these timbers must be all the same in depth and have a known load

22

bearing capability (in as far as this can be known where wood is concerned). Chapter 6 has more information on this in the section on timber floors.

Hardcore

Everybody knows what hardcore is and has got a good supply all over their gardens in the form of stones, bits of bricks and the odd fragment of concrete. Unless you are going to build a very large workshop or have really diabolically soft ground you won't need very much of it — a layer approximately 50mm thick over the base area is all that is required. Big does not mean better in this material and stones up to approximately 20mm max. will be fine. If you get the kids to earn their pocket money by collecting it for you make sure that they have only picked up stones. Sticks and leaves etc. are definitely not welcome. If you need to buy it make sure it is 'clean' before letting the delivery guy dump it on your lawn.

Once the hardcore is laid it is usually 'blinded' with a layer of sand to protect the damp-proof membrane from punctures. That's why you need a reasonable spread of sizes of stones otherwise a lot of blinding sand will be needed to fill the gaps. Daft as it may seem, watering the hardcore helps to consolidate it so give it a good soaking as well.

Concrete

The other main material used in the construction is concrete and it may be useful to explain a little about this seemingly mundane material. Concrete is a mix of sand, stones (called aggregate) and cement; the sand and aggregate usually being bought pre-mixed as ballast in a 75% aggregate, 25% sand mix. It is generally available in two grades; medium, which has stones of 20mm and downwards, and coarse, which has stones up to 40mm in size. As far as we are concerned we only need to use medium ballast. A general purpose concrete is made from a mix of 5 parts ballast and 1 part cement by volume (or shovelful), and this mix is ideal for our purpose. If you want to increase the strength a bit just increase the cement content a little.

As can be seen from the mass of concrete jungles that surround us, it is a very popular building material, being cheap, very strong in compression and can be reinforced with steel rods for use in beams or highly loaded pillars. The only real problem with it is that it cannot be used unsupported without reinforcement. In fact, it is so weak in tension or shear that it may actually collapse under its own self weight, so make sure that it is only laid on top of a good, well compacted, foundation. If the foundation is solid clay or well tamped hardcore you only need a layer of concrete around 100mm thick. If the floor is being laid over an existing concrete path or patio you will get away with just 75mm.

Mortar and screed are variations of concrete but they don't have any aggregate in them although they often have additives to make them workable or self levelling. We won't be needing much mortar, so you can mix your own by adding one part cement to five parts of sand. Add a little water and just a squirt of washing-up liquid to act as a plasticiser. That will make it sticky and workable — just like the real stuff! Add just enough water to allow you to roll the mix into sausages.

Cement — the magic ingredient — is made from ground-up limestone (or chalk) to which is added silica, alumina, iron oxide and a few other chemicals. The mix is heated to red heat in a massive, slowly revolving, drum in a process called calcining. The heat converts the limestone into

23

a chemical reaction waiting to happen . . . and it will just as soon as it gets anywhere near moisture. There are several types of cement available but the best for our purpose is Ordinary Portland. Most others are for special applications and just cost more to buy.

A few tips about concrete:-

(1) It doesn't actually need any free water to harden as it can draw what it needs straight from the atmosphere. If it does go off in this way it is not that much weaker than a wet mix would be.

(2) Adding too much water will produce a very sloppy mix that is easy to level but the strength is adversely affected. Use the smallest amount of water consistent with a manageable mix for the strip foundations but, for the finished floor, use a slightly runnier mix to get a smooth top finish to stand on. Do this by laying the wetter mix and, after levelling it off, keep tamping it down to make the 'cream' rise. The cream is a cement rich layer of water which will glaze the surface and give a very good flat top. Don't overdo it though as the surface, once dried, will have a tendency to dust or craze when you walk on it. Stop playing with it the minute you have a smooth top surface. *This should not be done to either structural or external concrete as it will tend to spall through frost damage. Nor will it achieve full strength as mentioned earlier.*

(3) All normal construction floors are finished with a 50–75mm screed which gives a fine grained level finish to the floor. I did not follow convention in the case of my own workshop simply because a perfectly good finish can be obtained using fine concrete as described in (2) above. I doubt if many people would leave a bare concrete floor to work off anyway, so it doesn't really matter what the floor is actually made of so long as it is level and smooth.

(4) One of the floors described in Chapter 6 shows rough sawn timber all around the inside of the perimeter walls. It is set dead level and with the top edge of the finished floor level. This traps the damp-proof membrane and gives a level to work to. I have this in my own floor and it makes levelling all round the edges very easy indeed. The timber does not have to be fixed in any way apart from a good jammed fit. This can be done on any of the floors.

(5) Concrete doesn't harden all at once. Initial hardening starts after about 3 hours and it continues until full hardness is reached after about 28 days. For this reason be very careful with your green concrete as damage is almost impossible to repair properly.

(6) For good concrete that will achieve its full strength it is very important to protect it both from drying out too rapidly and from being exposed to frost. Both will cause premature cracking and early failure. If you lay it in summer when it is relatively hot cover it as soon as you have finished and, if necessary, damp it down after the first 'set'. Always cover concrete if you lay it in winter, even if it has been down for a couple of days, as it will still have a tremendous amount of free water in it which will freeze given half a chance. (It would pay you to cover it anyway as a Fundamental Law states that as soon as anyone lays any concrete a cat will materialise and walk right across it!)

Finally on the subject of concrete; where to get it? Once again you will find it difficult to beat the offers made for cement and ballast in your local paper's small ads. Work out the quantities of each ingredient by using the data in the Appendix and then get on the phone. Another good reason for buying the materials this way is because the price invariably includes delivery. If you build the removable base then you don't need much concrete and it may be worth buying the pre-bagged, pre-mixed stuff from your local DIY store. You will, however, still need a fair amount of sand and a bag or two of cement.

Sand

There are two types of sand; fine (builders) and coarse (sharp). Fine sand, which is usually yellow, is used for making mortar and rendering and the result is a very brittle material because of the lack of decent particle sizes in the mixture. Coarse sand is used for floor screeds and paving slabs and has larger particles which increase the mixture strength quite dramatically. The bigger the particle size the bigger the compressive strength.

The only point to watch with sand is the quality. Rub some of it between your fingers and no serious staining should result. Dirty sand, often caused by clay contamination, makes very poor mortar which is liable to spall in winter because the contaminant holds water which subsequently freezes.

Pea shingle

Pea shingle is what the name implies – pea-sized stones. You will only need to get some if you intend to dig a soakaway or run a land drain.

Membranes

The membranes are an essential part of the building. Leave them out or fail to install them correctly and you risk permanent troubles.

There are three membranes in a building and, if the detailing is correct, they can all be made from the same material. They are:

(1) **DPC** This is the damp-proof course and it is built into walls at a point approximately 150mm above ground level. It's there to stop damp rising or 'wicking' up the wall from the water table below. Normally sold as a thin plastic strip with both sides ridged for grip and is laid in a bed of mortar between two brick courses.

In the base for this workshop this strip membrane can be replaced by an extension to the floor damp-proof membrane as shown.

(2) **DPM** The damp-proof membrane is a sheet of relatively thin plastic which is laid on top of the groundworks before the floor proper is laid. Its purpose is to isolate the internal floor from any water which may be around it. The process known as 'tanking out' performs a similar function but really applies when the floor is below the surrounding ground level.

(3) **Vapour barrier** This is a continuous plastic sheet that is built into the walls and its purpose is to prevent the migration of moisture into the building via the upper structure. Thinner polythene is suitable for this service but it must be fitted carefully – and at the right point in the wall (and occasionally the roof) – for it to be fully effective.

The sheeting is available in two thicknesses – grade 1000 which is the heavy duty stuff and grade 500 which is thinner. Always try to use the 1000 grade for the

DPM in the base or, if you find it too difficult to manage or fold properly, two sheets of 500 grade on top of each other will do just as well. Use 500 grade for the vapour barrier.

The membrane materials are available quite cheaply from most DIY stores and builders' merchants so there shouldn't be a problem getting it. The width available locally is 4m and it is bought 'off the roll' so you can have any length that you need. Don't worry about trying to get a continuous skin around the wall or floor as joints can be made simply by overlapping. (The fitting of these materials is covered in detail in the relevant chapters.)

You can purchase the DPM in a tin either in the form of bituminous paint or as a liquid silicon solution which effectively waterproofs concrete. Both are OK but they do rely on nothing moving – ever. By moving I do not mean by any detectable amount – even a hairline crack could be enough to allow water to penetrate. I favour the visible polythene liner because it can be checked easily for damage just before laying the floor.

Door and windows
Good quality doors and windows are essential for a satisfactory job, but if you are not careful buying them will give your wallet the worst battering it's had since last Christmas! I cannot overstress the importance of a good sound door because it is the obvious way in for any thief and is often the weakest part of the whole structure. The problem is that a good new one is going to cost a lot of money – and then you need a decent frame to put it in. Windows are another weak point so they should either be too small to get through or of very high quality. It's getting more expensive by the minute!

Actually, with a little searching, it need

not be too bad. Once again try looking in your local paper, especially for second-hand double-glazed units as they are often almost impenetrable, but make sure that you get the door frame as part of the deal. If you don't fancy double-glazed units or can't find any, there are three other possible sources which you can try before going out and buying new ones:

(1) Double-glazing firms. Go along to a local outlet, or, if you know where it is, the local depot and seek out the foreman. It is worth paying a reasonable amount for the assembly as the frame at least would normally be destroyed during removal. This is because it would have been built into the wall using metal cramps which must be cut through to release the frame. Normally they would simply saw through the frame and rip it out in pieces.

(2) Next on the list is a demolition site. Be very clear about what you want though – you need a garage side door or a house back door, complete with frame, and it must be hardwood. *If you don't explain this at the start and then try to argue the toss later, you could find that you don't need a workshop by the time they've finished with you!*

(3) Last on the list and the most expensive, short of buying new, is the salvage yard. These places specialise in the recycling of things like old fireplaces, cast iron baths etc., but they also hold reasonable value items like doors.

I would suggest that once you've decided to build a workshop you start looking immediately for the door, windows and cheap sources of timber. It could take some time to find them but it will be worth it. Incidentally, if your workshop is going to be on the compact side then an outward opening door will probably be best but it may not be easy to find one. Garage side doors are often handed this way but house doors usually open inwards. Don't worry too much about this point though, as the handing can be changed with a little effort and ingenuity – it's just more work.

Internal lining

This workshop derives its strength from the way that the walls are constructed. They each form box beams that are immensely strong and relatively light. The beam is formed by securely attaching a sheet of wood to one side of a stud-wall frame and then closing the other side with conventional strip cladding in such a way that it too forms the equivalent of a sheet material. There are plenty of suitable materials to choose from for lining the inside but select with care and bear in mind what you are likely to hang on it. For a simple skin, that will not be loaded, you can use 6mm ply. For higher loadings choose 12mm blockboard, 12mm chipboard or, if your purse will stretch to it, 15mm high density chipboard. I must admit that I would not recommend plasterboard or very thin ply because they cannot carry any decent shelf loadings and may well prove to be a nuisance later. There is also a tremendous selection of faced boards available but it would also be best to avoid these as they can encourage condensation on the machinery and equipment inside by stopping the building from 'breathing'. (For further information on the subject of condensation and its control see my article Vapour Trouble published in the *Model Engineer*, May to September 1993).

If for some reason you need water in your workshop, especially if it's an extension of the mains supply, avoid using chipboard unless you can guarantee you will never have a leak. When it gets wet – it swells by around 50% of its original size – it will not return to normal even when dry. Use blockboard or plywood instead, but ensure that the lining falls short of the floor by at least 12mm. The skirting can, of course, make contact as it should survive a soaking.

External cladding

The external cladding can be whatever takes your fancy as several types are available. Probably the most common is weatherboard; a wedge-shaped plank of somewhat low grade wood often used for garden sheds and fences. At the other end of the scale is shiplap which is an interlocking planking that has a pleasant profiled section. Weatherboard is cheap but tends to be very 'knotty' and has a strong tendency to warp and split unless it is securely fixed at very frequent intervals. Shiplap is more expensive but is thicker, and therefore more stable, and the interlocking of the planks gives a stronger, more weatherproof walling.

There are two other materials which you can use. The first is tongue and groove, which is more usually used for internal wall lining, but it can be used externally providing a heavy grade is used. The other is exterior grade plywood and I would use this if I was intending to paint the finished workshop.

With the obvious exception of plywood, most cladding materials are available in two widths: 100mm and 150mm. Don't bother with the 100mm stuff, buy the bigger size as it is more economical and has superior longitudinal stability.

Roofing materials

To keep the design simple a mono-pitch roof of shallow angle has been designed, but an alternative pitched design is also given for the more adventurous builder. The simple roof type is easy to build and is completely satisfactory providing reasonable workmanship and decent materials are used. I would only use exterior grade plywood for this job as any other sheet material is likely to warp and disintegrate if water ever gets to it; it's one thing to replace the roof covering, but it's no joke if you have to replace the roof as well! The plywood does not have to be very thick if you construct the roof as designed and providing you treat it with respect if ever you need to climb on it. You then need to cover the whole roof. (There is one material which, in theory at least, could be used without any covering at all apart from a coat of varnish — marine plywood. Very expensive and quite difficult to find inland, it is totally waterproof and ideal for the job.)

Roof coverings

There are three choices of covering: painted rubber, mineral felt and butyl sheeting.

Painted rubber There are a whole host of these finishes around now and your local DIY centre will probably have several types on the shelf. They are neat and very convenient to use as they are water soluble — but not when dry of course. My own workshop is painted with this type of material.

Mineral felt This can also be bought from any DIY shop or builders' merchant, but it must be fitted correctly for it to have a reasonable life — around 10 years.

Butyl sheeting This is ideally suited to a simple square roof which is completely flat. Butyl 'overcoats' are made up by specialist companies to your dimensions and are made slightly small so they stretch on fitting. Expensive to buy but this covering will outlive all others. Look in your local trade directory for a supplier. All of these

materials, together with fitting instructions, are covered in detail in Chapter 7.

Insulation

Insulation is required in three places — the walls, floor and the roof. Luckily someone has invented a single material which satisfies the needs of each location. It's called extruded polystyrene and you will find it at builders' suppliers (but probably not at your local DIY shop). It is made in all sorts of thicknesses for just about every insulation situation and is so dense that it can even be laid in the floor and concreted over. Water will not affect it. The sheets can be cut very easily — unlike earlier types which just broke up into balls when cut — and they can be made a nice snug fit in the framing. Don't confuse this material with the polystyrene that is used in moulded form in domestic appliance packaging.

Alternatively there is a compacted form of roof insulation — rock fibre or glass fibre in sheets — and they too can be cut quite easily. *Remember though that glass fibre is a respiratory irritant and a face mask must be worn when handling it.*

General items

The only other items that you need are general ironmongery, which is probably best purchased as the need arises; woodscrews — plain steel for inside, brass in contact with damp; plated or Japanned for external use; and galvanised nails for external use.

Removable floor materials

For those people who do not want to leave a concrete slab behind when they remove the workshop a design is shown in Chapter 6 for a removable floor. Even though it is temporary its construction includes all of the waterproofing fitted to the permanent floor. This floor and its surround can be lifted and moved if required and only the shallow strips of concrete foundation will be left behind. If the base is constructed according to the design given these strips should be below the ground anyway. (Take a look at the sketch of this floor in Chapter 6.)

In order to achieve the portability aspect some materials are specified which would normally be associated with a patio. One such item is the kerbing which is used both to contain the floor slabs and as a perimeter wall to build the walls off. Kerbing is profiled concrete of immense strength and is available from builders' suppliers in various profiles. You can mould your own or you could shutter the foundation concrete during construction to get the same profile – providing you don't mind leaving it behind of course.

The floor is made up of either concrete paving slabs or standard garden patio slabs. Try to avoid slabs less than 50mm thick and, for economy, try to get 600mm square or larger ones. This type of floor will almost certainly be covered so I wouldn't worry about the colour if you can't find plain ones. They can be purchased from DIY centres and builders' merchants but before going there look in your local paper for cheaper sources of supply. The only thing that you must check when buying is that they are flat. Any that were taken out of the casting box too soon after manufacture will be curved.

Right, you've got the tools; there's a big pile of ballast on the lawn; the garden has been picked clean of stones and there's a couple of bags of cement threatening to go off in the shed. Get your wellies on – it's time to start . . .

CHAPTER 5

Groundworks and rainwater drains

Groundworks

By now you should know exactly how big the workshop will be and where it is going to be built. If you are also a gardener you will know what type of subsoil you have, but if you're not, scrape off the top layer on the chosen spot and take a good look at it. You need to know because it affects the amount of work that will have to be done before the base can be laid. You should find out if it is hard or soft and whether it is wet or dry. Generally, clay and chalk are good substrata material but loam or sandy soil are not so good. Don't worry if the subsoil is soft because the ground loading of the structure is very low and subsidence or shift should not occur providing the correct steps are taken at the outset. The 'correct steps' amount to spending extra time compacting the trench bottoms and then pouring in hardcore, followed by more thumping, followed by more hardcore . . .

It is important that you remove the topsoil — even if it appears to be well compacted — as it will contain degradable vegetable matter which could cause any structure built on it to crack or sink. The same material is attractive to insects so ants, worms and various other nasties will burrow in it. On a small structure like this

The perfect situation — secluded, adjacent to the house and on hard stony ground.

it could lead to soil migration on a surprising scale. (Those of you that have built patios on a simple thin bed of sand laid straight on top of levelled topsoil will know exactly what I mean.)

If the workshop is to be built within the bounds of an estate-type development, you will almost certainly find that when the houses were built all of the original topsoil was scraped off and set aside. On completion of construction the contractor would then have replaced the topsoil on the garden areas to a depth of about 225mm, while also losing a couple of tons of broken bricks and concrete in the process! Providing subsequent owners of the property haven't done any double digging, the subsoil should still be quite well compacted. In such cases the dividing line between topsoil and subsoil is usually quite easy to detect, but for those who can't find the dividing line, somewhere between 150mm and 225mm will be OK. An area that is already heavily compacted, such as part of an existing patio or a section of an established hard-worn lawn, is an ideal location. In cases like this the subsoil layer will only be a few centimetres below the surface and you could practically lay the base straight on the ground after removing the grass layer.

Before you can start excavating you need to know which type of floor you are going to lay as it affects the groundworks. There are five basic types described in this book so everyone should be able to find one that suits their pocket, ability etc. Briefly, the five types are:

Simply supported timber floor
Suspended timber floor
Concrete floor over an existing slab
Removable base
Standard concrete base

They are all covered in detail in Chapter 6 and I would suggest that you have a look at the drawings there and decide which type suits you if you don't already know. The same drawings also show the extent of groundworks for each type of base. Two of them don't require any real groundworks as such, but that doesn't mean that you can skip the rest of this chapter because the service trench and drain have got to be put in yet.

At long last you can actually do something – the digging! While this may not be your favourite activity, in this context it is very rewarding because you will finally see your future workshop taking shape 'in the solid' so to speak. The very first thing to do is to level the whole base area plus a strip of about 300mm around the perimeter. If the ground undulates always pare it down to a level site before digging out for the foundations rather than infilling the low points as this could lead to a soft spot later. Similarly, on a sloping site, always cut into the slope rather than build up to a level surface. Get it as level as you can as it will help you to get the foundation strip top edge nice and level ready to take the perimeter walls. (If you do not like the idea of laying bricks you can extend the foundation strips upward to include the walls. Even so, it will still be useful to start with a level site.) Next, peg out the area of the base and don't be surprised if what looked quite a large area on paper suddenly looks very small in reality. I don't know why this is but it's true of all floor areas – just visit a building site and look at the bare floor slabs. It seems hard to believe that a whole house could be built on such a small patch but when the house is completed it looks correctly proportioned.

In theory you planned everything right down to the last detail before ever going near your spade. So, all you should need to do now is dig the trenches and bung the foundations in. Typically, nothing is ever straightforward. There are some minor refinements that can be considered 'on the way'. One such is — what will be around the outside? If it will be, or already is, lawn, then cutting the grass up against the workshop wall is going to be a nuisance. If you extend the width of the foundations by about 150mm outwards there will be somewhere for the lawnmower to run onto and you will always get the edges. What about access? You could lay a simple flagstone path with the slabs just laying on the ground, or, you might want a proper concrete path. Decide on these items now, reset your pegs and dig out accordingly.

There isn't much to say about the digging, except that it's hard work! If the ground is dry and hard, set the sprinkler on it the night before for a couple of hours to soften it up a bit. Pull a line between the pegs and use a good spade to cut along the edges of the trenches. Trick the kids into getting the spoil out and then use the spade to level off the trench and floor bottoms. As you approach the depth required try not to go too deep, but if you do, backfill the excess depth with compacted hardcore and not soil. When the whole thing is trenched out take your tamper and give the bottoms a good thumping until they are good and firm. If hard tamping simply leads to an ever-increasing trench depth (soft ground) throw in some hardcore and tamp it well down until the depth is about correct.

Your plan will have included sorting out the route and point of entry of the power cable and any other services. If they are to be run below ground you must make suitable entry points for them before pouring the concrete foundation strips. Electricity is very nasty stuff because you can't see it, smell it, or even tell how powerful it is. There is always the danger that some time later you may decide to plant a tree having forgotten all about it. *It is very important that you run the power cable in accordance with the following instructions* — then you will know that it is safely out of harm's way. Underground cables must be below spade depth and either encased in a pipe (or conduit) and/or covered by a run of edging stones. 22mm plastic water pipe is ideal for the encasement and it should be laid in a narrow trench not less than 450mm deep. *Be absolutely sure to fix some durable indication that there is a power cable underground — not only for your own information but also for those that follow you.*

At the point where it will rise up through the workshop floor use a suitable bend and a short vertical piece to bring the top of the pipe to around 50mm above the finished floor level. The pipework should be assembled using the correct proprietary glue so that the whole run is watertight. If you don't run the cable at the same time thread strong twine through it for pulling the cable through later. At this stage you only need to worry about the workshop end — you can trench the lawn out later. The conduit will be below the bottom of the foundations in many cases but I would suggest that where the trench passes underneath the foundation strip, concrete is used to backfill it. (If you are constructing the removable floor try to ensure that the cable emerges right in the corner so that you can just bevel the corner of a slab to accommodate it.)

A similar arrangement should be made if a water supply is required with the exception that it should be laid below frost level in a trench at least 900mm deep (that's UK frost level — if you live somewhere colder, check the depth it should be run at). It would be prudent to run both services in the same trench of course and I would suggest that you lay and test the complete water pipe run before burying it, just in case! You can then backfill the trench to 450mm deep ready for the power cable.

Don't put the spade away yet because the digging isn't finished – not if you need a drain that is . . .

Rainwater drains

Here in Britain we have an ancient law which makes it illegal for a property owner to allow drips to fall on passers-by. Believe it or not this is the origin of eavesdropping. (Presumably in the days before gutters were fitted people used to stay very close to the house walls in order not to be dripped on, which meant that they could then hear all that was said inside the building.) From this comes our obsession with gutters, drains, and downpipes. As far as I know, no other countries have the same law so they very often don't bother on all but the largest buildings, but the good old Brits put gutters around everything – including the shed! (I think the law stems from medieval times when people used to empty bedpans out of the window to the detriment of the ladies in their finery below!)

Do you really need a drain at all? If you consider that the water would have fallen on the ground and just soaked in anyway then you probably don't. The amount of water is the same – it just all appears in one spot instead of spread out. All that you really need to do is build the roof with a generous overhang so the water drops to the ground rather than running down the walls and forget all about it – providing it doesn't drop on a public highway or path of course.

If only life was so simple! In my case the access path down the side of the house also runs along the workshop front, so some means of getting rid of the water was needed. In relation to a small workshop there are four methods worth considering:

(a) **Guttering to a safe spot where the water can be discharged**
(b) **Guttering into a waterbutt**
(c) **Guttering into a downpipe and then into a soakaway**
(d) **Guttering into a downpipe and then to an existing rainwater open gully**

Only options (c) and (d) need any real explanation but there are some points on the first two that are worth stating:

(a) Channelling the water to, say, a fruit tree or a fish pond is a good idea, but make sure that you are not just storing up a problem for later. Water is a nuisance if it gets where you don't want it – even more so when it freezes – so do be sure that wherever it ends up it will be acceptable for as long as the workshop exists.

(b) A waterbutt is an excellent idea. Stand the container on a pile of bricks and be sure to make a cover to go over the top or mosquitoes will breed in the water. It will also avoid the problem of finding a dead cat in it one day. Waterbutts freeze over in winter so stop the downpipe above the water level or it will freeze and your guttering will be useless as there will be no way out for the water. Remember though – if you don't draw the water off regularly you will end up with the full flow going down the overflow; which you would fit wouldn't you? During winter you are not likely to so the overflow must be led to somewhere suitable as in (a) above.

The other two need a little more explanation:

(c) Soakaway

I decided on a soakaway as the best solution to my water disposal problem. It's more hard work and the result is a big hole in the ground and yet another pile of soil to get rid of somewhere — but at least I don't have to worry about a water surplus.

The idea is to provide a large surface area of ground which is capable of absorbing the full flow without clogging or swamping itself. Detail 5.1 shows the essential elements of a soakaway. Actually, you don't need that big a hole, and for the sort of roof area that we are talking about around a half a cubic metre will be quite adequate for most ground conditions. In very free draining ground, such as chalk, you only need a little reception box of, say, 300mm cubed. These holes must be buried of course, and a covering of around 300mm is needed on top. That gives us a hole 500mm × 500mm × 800mm deep for normal ground and 300mm × 300mm × 600mm for chalky or sandy ground. The water pipe leads in

close to the top so if the soakaway is dug some way from the workshop you must make allowance for the fall of the pipe in the depth of the hole. The pipe fall can be very shallow (for plastic piping) but should not be less than 20mm over 1000mm. This means that the soakaway can be up to 15 metres away before you need to increase the 300mm top covering dimension.

When you have dug the hole fill it with stones, bits of bricks, surplus hardcore etc. If the stones are big and the resulting interstices are quite large, fill in the gaps with pea shingle as you put the stones in. This will stop the soil in the walls of the hole leeching in and clogging the whole thing up. Feed the water pipe in at the top, lay a flat stone over it to protect it from material collapsing from above and surround it with shingle to produce a level surface. All that remains to do then is to

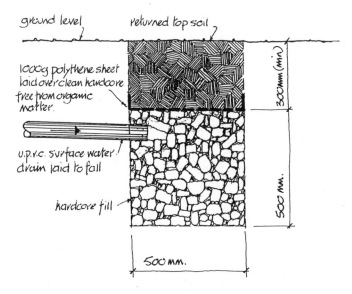

Detail 5.1 *Section through surface water soakaway.*

34

lay a piece of spare DPM approximately 200mm bigger all round to cover the stones and then backfill with soil. Now you can forget all about the water problem. *(Make a mental note though to fit a debris screen at the top of the downpipe to stop leaves etc. getting down the pipe and blocking the soakaway.)*

(d) Using an existing drain

Many houses have the rainwater downpipes led to open gullies set beside the walls where the water is then led either into a storm drain or a soakaway. It may be possible for you to lead your pipe into one of these either above or below ground level. In some cases the house drains are

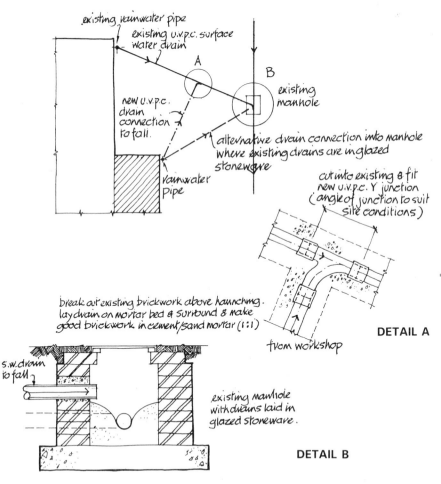

Detail 5.2 *Connecting into existing surface water drain circuits.*

commoned up at a manhole and you could possibly break in there. There are two types of manhole; moulded plastic and brick built. The plastic type, which are round, are easy to break into as they have capped spigots moulded all around the outside so that all you have to do is dig down the side until you find a spigot and then connect onto it. Alternatively, because the pipework is invariably plastic, it is perhaps easier to just cut into the pipe-run and fit a swept tee. Brick-built man-holes, which are usually square, are a bit more tricky because the pipes will be salt glazed stoneware which should not be messed about with. The only way to add an entry is to break through the brickwork and concrete in a new one. If you do break into a brick one, chop the hole from *inside* the manhole and make sure it isn't a foul drain — they are best left well alone! Detail 5.2 shows the various ways of adding the entries.

Land drainage

All of the foregoing just about covers the options for getting rid of rainwater but what if the ground itself waterlogs? There are many regions in England and Wales where the water table is often higher than ground level at times! If the high water table is a problem over the whole area then all you can do is try to break into the stormwater drains. If, however, the water problem is caused by a local topographical condition (such as a clay 'bowl') then maybe you could install a land drain. While this is really beyond the scope of this book a short description will not go amiss.

For a land drain to work there must be a lower level or a more porous soil to pipe the water to — a ditch, a drain or a chalky area for example. If these conditions can be met, dig a trench which starts at about 300mm deep and drops 20mm for every 1000mm until it reaches the discharge point. Put a 50mm layer of pea shingle in and then lay a 100mm diameter land drain pipe along the trench. (A land drain pipe is a purpose-made plastic pipe with small holes or slits cut through the wall which allows water to penetrate and flow away.) Surround the pipe with a further 50mm of pea shingle and then backfill the trench with soil.

There is another solution to the problem of ground water — trees, especially water-loving varieties such as willows. I believe that they can shift around 3000 litres an hour of water from their roots to a point 10 metres up in the air where it evaporates off. That's some pump! Don't be tempted to plant one within 10m of the workshop though — it could drastically alter the ground condition and cause severe shrinkage of clay soil. Similarly, be very careful about cutting down an established tree and building on or next to where it stood. The ground condition could change to a point where partial or complete saturation by water leads to an upthrust or 'heave', causing severe damage to adjacent buildings.

Before leaving the groundworks I will just add that when I built my workshop I dug a soakaway at the end which would later be the extension. This meant that the basic ground clearance was already done for when I built the extension. To make use of the space and to force compaction I laid heavy paving slabs on a thin layer of sand/cement over the area and sunk two 100mm square posts at the far corners. I then extended the workshop roof over it with clear plastic roofing to provide a very useful winter drying area. I would point out though that when I wanted the area for the extension I had to do the same again at the 'new' end of the workshop — *and guess where I'd dumped all of the soil from the ground-works!*

CHAPTER 6

The base and floor

If any part of the building is more important than any other it must be the base. Once it is down and everything else has been built on top it will be very difficult to correct mistakes or make repairs. So, take great care on this part and it should outlive you. The first part of the process was covered in the previous chapter on the groundworks: *only when you are sure that you have a good solid foundation should you start on the base itself.*

Of all the chapters this has been the most difficult to write, not because the subject is complicated, but because there are so many ways of preparing suitable bases that there is a real danger of creating confusion. The problem is that I feel I must show as many as possible so that every builder will find one that suits. There are five basic designs, two for timber floors and three for concrete. Then there are the variations on a theme; the bases built over existing slabs being a good example. The important thing for the builder to do is to study the drawings, understand the basic principles and then, with a bit of mix-n-match if necessary, build a base that suits the location and duty. It should be borne in mind that in building design nothing is set in concrete (sorry about that!). You could, for instance, cast a large concrete raft and then build off that rather than mess about with trenches etc. etc. Alternatively, you may decide to build a removable workshop but standing on a new fixed base.

The five designs are:

(1) **Detail 6.1**
Simply supported timber floor
(2) **Detail 6.2**
Suspended timber floor
(3) **Details 6.3, 6.4 & 6.5**
Floors built onto existing bases
(4) **Detail 6.6**
Removable base
(5) **Detail 6.7**
Standard concrete base

These 5 designs can be split into two obvious sections – timber and concrete. There are some notes which are common to both types and others which relate to only one or the other. I'll start with the common ones and the specific notes will appear under the relative headings later.

General notes

Floor elevation
Whichever base type is used the top of the floor should end up around 150mm above

the surrounding ground level. This will ensure that exceptional weather conditions don't flood your floor and also allows the groundworks under it to remain reasonably dry. A further, simpler reason for lifting the floor up is because you expect it to be elevated. If it isn't you may well stumble on your way in!

Invalid access

The exception to this is where a floor at ground level is necessary to allow access for the infirm or wheelchair-bound users and the drawback of possible localised flooding will have to be accepted. In these cases the perimeter wall should be left out in the door area and the floor laid at or near ground level. Building a true timber floor at ground level means a big hole to take the joists and to allow the required ventilation so I would suggest that this floor is avoided and you use a concrete one as shown in Detail 6.8 instead. Read the notes that go with the detail carefully (in the section on concrete floors) as there are a few complications.

Wall elevation

The lifting of the timber part of the building well above ground level is crucial to the longevity of the building fabric. This point cannot be overstressed as any failure to observe it will quickly lead to the degeneration of the lower timber members. Further protection is provided by the overlapped weatherboard which is positioned all around the bottom of the timber walls and protects both the DPC and the lower members of the walls from direct weather penetration.

Now that I've covered the prelims we can look at the bases themselves and the notes that are specific to them.

Timber floors

I have to make an admission here; much

as I like timber as a construction material, I am definitely not keen on its use for floors in this kind of base because as I mentioned earlier wood, water and soil definitely do not mix. So, taking into account my opposition to timber floors, why have I included a design in the book? The answer is that for some applications a shed-on-legs arrangement as shown by the simply supported timber floor (Detail 6.1) is ideal and many hobbyists will use this design. Then there are those who definitely want a proper timber floor as nothing else will do and who am I to argue? Herewith are two floor designs complete with the sort of detailing that should be included to protect them from early failure.

Wood and water

The floor, not surprisingly, is at the bottom of the building – right where all the water ends up – so this part of the structure takes the worst of the prevailing conditions from ground splashes, run-off and residual groundwater. Timber has a natural water content of around 15% and will survive for a very long time if this can be maintained. There are two conditions which must be met to achieve this: avoidance of excessive water contact and continuous and unimpeded ventilation of the timber sections. With correct detailing and construction wetting of the floor structure can be avoided and the timber, if given good ventilation, will always dry to a more or less stable condition and should have a very long life. In both of the floors shown the detailing is designed to eliminate any direct water penetration into the structure, but any subsequent damage in this area could soon lead to water finding its way into the ends of the floor joists and then into the floor itself. Wet softwood can have a life shorter than 6 months – so if you don't notice it quickly you could be in for a major letdown!

The need to adequately ventilate the underfloor void means that timber floors usually end up set higher than conventional concrete floors. This is especially true for the full suspended floor because of the joist thicknesses which have to be used. For most people this will not be too much of a problem but if you are infirm or confined to a wheelchair then a timber floor is probably not for you.

Damp-proof membrane

That's easy on the plain timber floors — there isn't one. There is still a damp-proof course on the joint between the wall and the floor though. However, if you add a layer of underfloor insulation, a DPM must be installed as condensation can occur between the wood and insulation layers and the floor could rot out. The position of the DPM is shown in Detail 6.2 but it applies just as equally to the simple timber floor shown in Detail 6.1.

The wallplate

Both the timber floors shown are sitting on a wallplate. This is a length of timber set dead level (normally on a bed of mortar) to provide a good point to build off. This does mean that the actual joint is weak because mortar doesn't bond to wood very well. It doesn't matter because the weight of the completed structure will keep it from leaving home but this weakness should be recognised during construction and looked after accordingly. The 'shed-on-legs' arrangement as shown in Detail 6.1 just relies on its own weight to keep in place although I'm sure that most people will devise some method of fixing it to the ground. In the case of the full suspended floor as per Detail 6.2 you can either screw the wallplate directly to the bricks with the membrane trapped underneath, or use galvanised cramps as

shown. Space the screws or cramps about 1.5m apart. If you drill down into the wall through the wallplate squirt a drop of non-setting mastic into the hole before inserting the rawlplug to maintain the integrity of the DPC and only use brass, galvanised, or stainless steel screws for this job.

On the timber floors the width of the wallplate is independent of the wall thickness and it means that 50mm, 75mm or 100mm studwork can be used without having to adjust the width at the wallplate to perimeter wall junction as happens on the concrete base versions. To see what I mean compare Details 6.2 and 6.7.

Floor loadings

There is a little problem with wood — it's not like steel with a predictable and closely bound molecular structure. It's a natural fibrous material with a characteristic that most other materials do not possess — short- and long-term loading differences. If a timber floor which is supported on joists has a heavy load placed on it, it might appear to be perfectly able to support the load without bowing. It would seem reasonable then that it would always be so — but it might not! The reason is that when the load is first placed the floor is subjected to a short-term load which it can carry without noticeable deflection. The trouble is that over time the timbers may adopt a new shape and the floor will deflect, possibly even to the point of failure. This effect can sometimes be seen on the ridge of a tiled roof where the ridge board dips in between the rafters. The roof would not have been built like it. So, if you do decide on a timber floor, consider carefully what sort of loading it will be subjected to and, if necessary, compensate for this by using deeper or more closely spaced joists, or by means of a spine wall.

Spine walls

A spine wall is an intermediate wall which is built up from a third foundation strip and supports the joists at mid span. They are very useful because they can be used to halve the depth of the joists for a given span, allow a far greater load on a given joist size, or double the allowable span of a given joist size. As it is very easy to build an additional wall while laying the base, I would put one in for a wood floor over 2m wide as a matter of course. The wall should be built to the same detail as the edge walls shown in Detail 6.2.

Joist selection

Most of the timber used in the construction can be ordinary run-of-the-mill material that can be bought from DIY shops or any timber yard but floor joists are different. They must be of good quality and all the same thickness or your floor will be uneven. Even for the simple floor you should buy wood to the following specifications:

(a) Only buy timber for joists from a reputable timber merchant and tell him the use it is intended for.

(b) Order 'S3' grade and ask the merchant to make sure that it is regularised (all the same depth).

(c) It is advisable on structural members such as this to buy timber that has been pressure impregnated with preservative. It costs a little more but it does give extra protection.

(d) Despite having made it known what the timber is for always inspect it closely just in case the merchant isn't as reputable as you thought. Look for splitting, shakes (wavy along the length), twists, loose knots, excessive number of knots and waney edges (where the sizer has cut into a knot or the timber is from the very outside of the tree near the bark). Reject any that is not to your liking.

(e) All structural timber is covered by BS 4471 and BS 5268 so if your timber complies with these then it should be fine — but check just in case.

Insulation

Some of you may have immediately noticed a problem — the wind will whistle under the floor and it will be very cold indeed. You should never fully enclose timber so you can't sheet over the underside of the joists after packing the spaces with insulation as dry rot may well appear. All that can be done (apart from laying reasonably thick carpet inside) is to fit polystyrene insulation between the joists as shown in Detail 6.2 but note that a vapour barrier must also be installed between the joists and the floor sheeting. *So the decision as to whether to insulate or not must be made before the floor goes in.*

Application

The details of the timber floors show them built on their own foundations but they are eminently suitable for constructing over an existing concrete slab. Just make sure that the slab is stable and that the thickness is at least 100mm.

Detail 6.1 Simply supported timber floor

In Detail 6.1 you are basically looking at a shed on stub walls which only run along the length of the workshop and do not close in the ends. The detail shows the wall standing on what is effectively a drainage channel. The walls can be brick, concrete blocks or even old railway sleepers copiously treated with preservative. The foundation must be extremely well compacted and the finished walls must have their top surface dead level with each other. If you don't fancy what is effectively a loose base you can substitute the brick wall arrangement on concrete strip foundations as shown in Detail 6.2.

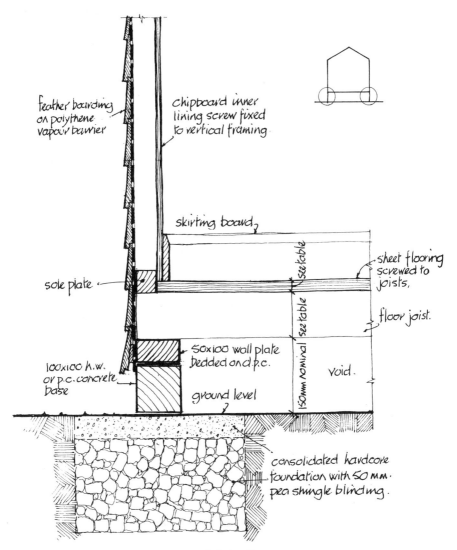

feather boarding on polythene vapour barrier

chipboard inner lining screw fixed to vertical framing

skirting board,

sole plate

sheet flooring screwed to joists,

floor joist.

50x100 wall plate bedded on d.p.c.

100x100 h.w. or p.c. concrete base

ground level

see table

150mm nominal see table

Void.

consolidated hardcore foundation with 50 mm. pea shingle blinding.

Detail 6.1 *Section through simply supported timber floor.*

41

The reason why there are just two parallel walls is because the underfloor area must be ventilated so the other two ends should be left open. To prevent the unsupported stub walls from toppling over when the kids use the side of the workshop as a safety wall during bike races, return the ends about 500mm or so, or make the ends of the walls into piers by doubling the wall thickness for a couple of brick lengths.

It must be remembered that this floor is a lightweight job and has been designed that way for maximum economy of materials and cost. It is ideally suited to a light duty such as aeromodelling or horology but there will be a certain 'springiness' in it if you start jumping up and down. The joists sizes, spacing and floor thickness for given spans are given in the following table.

LIGHTWEIGHT FLOOR MATERIAL SIZES

Span	Joist Size	Joist Spacing	Floor Thickness
m	mm	mm	mm
2	75 × 38	400	12
2.5	100 × 38	300	12
3	125 × 50	300	15

The floor derives its stiffness from the fact that the plywood is screwed down every 200mm or thereabouts *so it is very important that this is done*. If you build a spine wall, the sizes for the 2m span can also be used for the 3m span.

Finally, either treat the underfloor area of ground with a 'kill-all' weedkiller such as sodium chlorate or cover it with black polythene because you can bet your boots that an acorn or sycamore seed will be sitting in the ground just waiting for you to do something really stupid — like build over it!

Detail 6.2 Suspended timber floor

This is Detail 6.1's big brother — the Rolls-Royce of floors; expensive and quite difficult to build it will probably only be of interest to those people who own a timber yard or who are adamant that a proper timber floor is the only thing that we are meant to stand on! A slightly cheaper version would use plywood instead of proper floorboards. I must admit that this type of floor is very nice to stand on but much the same effect can be achieved at a far lower cost by laying a false timber floor over a concrete base as shown in Detail 6.9.

The depth of the joists and the need to ventilate the underside may well lead to a floor which is somewhat higher off the ground than any of the other types. In fact many buildings built with them require steps outside to gain access. Notice how the perimeter walls form a complete sub-base and that ventilation is achieved by air bricks spaced at about 1m intervals — so a 2m long wall will have 3 air bricks. They only need to be fitted in the two short walls and *must be kept clear at all times during the life of the building*.

This floor has been designed to deal safely with 'normal domestic loadings' which, for those who are interested are a dead load of 0.25 kn/sq.m (the self weight of the floor finish) and an imposed load of 1.5 kn/sq.m (the loading that is placed on the floor). This is the same as most suspended floors as found in domestic properties in the UK. The sizes are derived from a very sophisticated formulae — 'half the span in inches plus two inches'. Now, what's that in metric? It should be 1/12th of half the span in millimetres plus 50mm (or 1/24th of the span plus 50mm) doesn't have quite the same ring to it does it? This 'rule of thumb' applies with the standard joist spacing of 400mm; change the spacing and it changes the joist sizes.

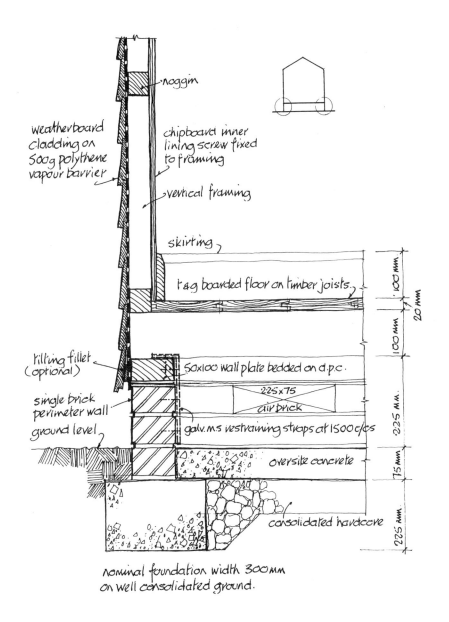

weatherboard
cladding on
500g polythene
vapour barrier

noggin

chipboard inner
lining screw fixed
to framing

vertical framing

skirting

t & g boarded floor on timber joists.

100 MM

20 MM

tilting fillet
(optional)

single brick
perimeter wall

ground level

50x100 wall plate bedded on d.p.c.

225 x 75
air brick

100 MM

galv. m.s restraining straps at 1500 c/cs

225 MM

oversite concrete

75 MM

consolidated hardcore

225 MM

nominal foundation width 300mm
on well consolidated ground.

Detail 6.2 *Section through suspended timber floor.*

43

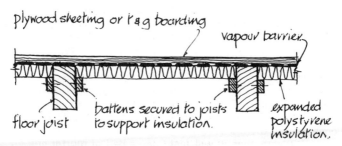

plywood sheeting or r$g boarding

vapour barrier

floor joist

battens secured to joists to support insulation.

expanded polystyrene insulation.

Detail 6.2 *Timber floor insulation.*

Anyway, to stop it from getting complicated and to save you the bother of working it out, Peter has knocked up another table of sizes with the numbers suitably adjusted for commonly available timber sizes.

SUSPENDED FLOOR MATERIAL SIZES

Span	Joist Size	Joist Spacing	Floor Thickness
m	mm	mm	mm
1.3	100 × 38	600	20
1.6	100 × 50	600	20
2	100 × 38	300	12
2	100 × 50	400	16
2	125 × 38	600	20
2.5	125 × 38	300	12
2.5	125 × 50	400	16
3	125 × 50	300	12
3	170 × 50	600	20

The apparently peculiar spans of 1.3m and 1.6m are given for those cases where a spine wall will be used and the span doubled. The table has enough of a selection to allow most people to match up the sizes with the timber available locally.

Proper floorboards are tongue and grooved so that they line up perfectly along the full length and they should really be installed in a state of compression. Builders achieve this by fixing the first

board down and positioning the next half dozen or so in place. A device called a cramp is then wedged between a convenient joist or noggin and the edge of the row of floorboards. Then they jack the whole lot together until the boards bow up from the joists whereupon the biggest builder on the site is told to jump on them while the carpenter bangs the nails in. In a self-build situation all you can do is to emulate the process as much as possible as follows: fix the first board nice and square to the wall and then slide the next one into the groove (or onto the tongue). Then, with a rubber or wooden mallet and a suitable small block of wood, really thump the board home along its length before nailing it down. The nails should be proper flooring nails (which have a slightly rounded head) and the heads should be punched in so that they are below the surface. Splay the nails slightly to prevent the boards from warping while they're down and fit a noggin where the ends of two boards meet.

Often modern suspended timber floors do not have floorboards as such at all. The 'boards' are large sheets of man-made boarding but with a tongue and groove along two edges as per normal flooring planks. By all means use these in place of planks and fix them by nailing as described. However, if you substitute plywood for the covering use at least 12mm thick sheets and note that ply does not like being nailed, so screw it down for a good job.

Concrete floors

I suspect you've already got the notion that I much prefer concrete as the material for the base and floor. There is no doubt that it is cheaper and there's something about it that suggests that it will last forever, unlike a timber floor which must succumb to the elements at some time. The bases illustrated should cover most eventualities but with a little thought they can be suitably modified to cope with any oddball situations which may arise.

A little time spent studying the illustrations will soon make it obvious to the non builder what is required. Foundation and base drawings often look a bit complicated when in fact they are just multi-ply structures like plywood – you just start at the bottom and work up. Fortunately it doesn't have to be done all in one go as each element can be built separately but try not to leave months between starting and finishing. A weekend could see most bases down but, in order for each part to attain some strength before being trampled on while building the next bit, it would be advisable to leave a three-day gap between each one. However, once you've started on any one part try to avoid stopping partway through – especially when laying the floor slab.

The essential elements of the design are the thickness of the base, the detailing of the DPM and DPC, the elevation of the floor level and the elevation of the wooden part of the building from the ground. Observe these points and all should be well.

The general notes given at the start of the chapter relate to concrete floors as well so make sure that you have read them. The following notes are specific to this type of floor and then there are a few more for each type of base.

Perimeter walls

Anyone who is already competent at bricklaying can skip this paragraph – because this is going to be a real Boy Scout's guide to the art! First, starting at a corner, lay a bed of mortar around 400mm long on the edge of the base and about 25mm deep. Take a brick, turn it frog down, then plop it onto the mortar and tap it level in two planes – ending up with a mortar joint around 8 to 10mm thick. (Bricks are normally laid frog up but seeing as we are only laying two courses and we want a nice flat top to put the wallplate on, they are best laid upside down.) Repeat the process at the opposite corner and then on the other two so you have a height line to work to all around the base. Tie a length of builder's line around the end of a brick and lay it across one of the laid bricks so that the line is in line with the outside edge of the brick – then tie another brick on the other end so the line can be pulled the full length of the workshop. All you've got to do then is fill the gap with bricks using the line as a guide. Go right round the workshop until you have a single course of bricks laid. Then start the second course but with the bricks lapped so the upper brick covers the joint between two lower ones. If that's all that you need to do then it would be so easy that we'd all be bricklayers – but you need mortar in the vertical joints (perpends) as well. When you've tried doing it you'll realise why we're not all bricklayers! It is very easy really. Just 'butter' the end of the brick with *exactly* the right amount of mortar so that you get a 10mm joint when it's squeezed against the next brick without pushing the first out of place. Or

45

The ground was so hard that very little hardcore was needed, hence the shallow floor depth. Note the strip foundations and the bricks laid frog down. The pipe is for a drain in the concrete area and leads to the soakaway.

The floor laid within the perimeter walls. You can just make out the wood strip used as a level against the brick wall. Note the drainpipe emerging into the soakaway in the foreground and the tee branch where the gutter downpipe will join onto. The walls are obscured by the DPC but are there!

you can stuff the mortar in afterwards as I did!

Damp-proof membrane
In most cases the membrane not only 'tanks' out the floor but it also doubles up as the damp-proof course in the walls. The object is simple — to stop the wet stuff from rising up and saturating the nice concrete that you've just broken your back laying! Take care to install it *exactly* as shown and with the correct overlap

with the vapour barrier and then you can completely forget about dampness. Never forget that it's there though, and not far down, so don't go and drill fixings straight into the floor! It is worth noting that just as the DPM keeps water out, it is just as good at keeping it in. Don't be in too much of a hurry to put the carpets down because it can take a very long time for the floor to dry out fully after construction. Watch out for leaks as well — even a small leak from say, a window frame, could

46

soon lead to a floor which is very wet, especially during the winter period when the ambient temperature is low.

Technically, the DPM and DPC should be separate items, thus avoiding the possible problem of the relatively thin DPM being damaged during the erection of the walls. They should also be bedded in mortar with a small overlap between them. Detail 6.7, the standard concrete base, shows this in a sub-detail so you can see how it should be done. In practice, the method advocated in this book of a nice flat perimeter wall top, a securely fixed wallplate, protection from direct exposure by the cladding overlap, and a little care, will result in a perfectly adequate DPC for the duty. If there is any doubt about the DPM's condition lay a strip of DPC on top of it just before you place the wallplate.

Reinforcement

Providing that you have prepared the groundworks properly you need not concern yourself with any thoughts of metal reinforcement in the floor slab. In fact, with the thickness being used it would not be wise to include any as it could actually weaken the whole thing.

Base thickness

As the kind of structure being used presents a relatively light load on the foundations and, because the floor loading will be relatively light, the thickness of the base has been minimised to 100mm and is adequate for a floor width of about 3m – providing it is laid on a firm base of compacted hardcore. *Under no circumstances reduce this figure*. However, if you are going to install quite a heavy mass, such as floor standing-machines with relatively small base areas, I would strongly suggest that you increase the thickness to 150mm.

Insulation

An insulation layer is actually shown in some of the details but its fitment is by no means obligatory. Just about all modern 'full-scale' floors have a layer of polystyrene foam built in as ground insulation and, if you intend to work off a bare concrete floor, it would be beneficial to include such a layer. I must admit that I didn't bother in my own workshop because the floor is covered by underlay and then vinyl flooring so it is indirectly insulated from inside anyway. If you intend to similarly cover the floor then by all means leave this item out.

The foam sheets are inexpensive and, because the finished floor level is to be 150mm above ground, it can be used as packing to save on hardcore or concrete, but don't use it to reduce the concrete thickness below 100mm. It's useful when positioned under the DPM as it prevents puncture of the membrane. In fact it is not really important as to exactly where it is and the details show it in various positions. So, you can put it wherever you like with just one limitation: if you intend to put it in the 'conventional' position i.e. on top of a rough concrete base and under a layer of floor screed, make sure that the screed thickness is at least 65mm and that a layer of 12mm mesh chicken wire is built into the screed for added strength.

One last point on insulation. As stated earlier in the timber floor section the addition of insulation encourages condensation so you have to add a vapour barrier to stop the moisture from appearing in the structure. When it is added in a concrete floor, there is a possibility of damp so the barrier *has to be fitted on the structure side of the insulation*, just the same as in the insulated timber floor. In some cases the insulation can be positioned below the DPM so it doubles as the vapour barrier – as shown in Detail 6.3. Detail 6.4

shows the additional vapour barrier when the insulation has to be installed above the DPM.

Removable walls

The description of the removable base (later in this chapter), describes a method of arranging for the removable walls to be screwed to the base, either by a wide soleplate or by casting cramps into the floor as shown in Detail 6.6. It is quite possible that some people may wish to erect a removable workshop but on a fixed base, in which case one of these two methods should be incorporated while building the base. A part-detail on Detail 6.4 shows how this can be achieved by leaving 'pockets' in the floor concrete and then grouting the cramp in later when the walls are up.

The base details

The bases which have brick perimeter walls all show the wall studwork as 50mm wide because, apart from being perfectly adequate for the job, building a 100mm wide wall is not cheap. However, the thicker wall does give a tidier arrangement at the wall/floor junction as shown in Detail 7.1 in Chapter 7. If you own a woodyard or just happen to have 30 or so 100mm × 50mm timbers lying around then by all means build to this detail. In most cases the walls will be fitted out with benches and floor-standing cabinets etc. so the little box-out at skirting level as shown in the illustrations will not show — not that it matters if it does.

Detail 6.3 Base built over existing concrete (1)

Using an existing slab must surely be the cheapest and easiest ways of building a base. It doesn't really matter if it is cracked as long as it has stopped settling. This and the next detail are for existing slabs

which are at ground level so there is a need to lift the floor up. This one shows an insulation layer being used as a convenient packing piece as well as the strips of wood used to hold the DPM in place around the perimeter wall. Be careful when fitting the strips; they should just be a light wedge fit — otherwise your nice new walls are likely to end up somewhere else!

Detail 6.4 Base built over existing concrete (2)

The two differences between this and Detail 6.3 are that the DPM is a bitumen based paint-on sealer and is therefore below the insulation, and the interior is screeded out to bring the floor level with the wallplate top. Ideally, paint on sealants should only be used on sound, uncracked concrete. Note the additional vapour barrier and the hooked cramp detail which is an alternative to drilling through the wallplate. The hook over the top should be used where high winds are normal, but most walls could be fixed by simple cramps which just rise up the side of the wallplate.

Detail 6.5 Base built over existing concrete (3)

Where the existing concrete base is already above ground level and the same size as the workshop will be, all that you have to do is lay the floor. The perimeter wall can be timber because the DPM goes underneath it, *but only when the workshop walls overhang the slab all around the edges. In any other circumstances the wall must be brick and the DPM run over the top as in Details 6.3 and 6.4.* Note that the floor is a screed rather than concrete and that if there is any doubt as to whether the base is nice and solid, it should have chicken-wire reinforcement biased towards the top rather than the

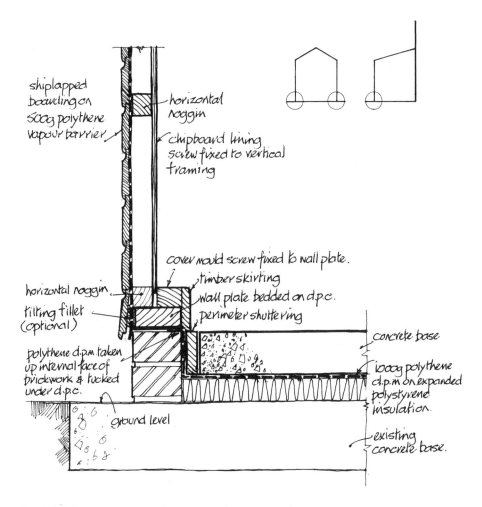

shiplapped boarding on 500g polythene vapour barrier

horizontal noggin

chipboard lining screw fixed to vertical framing

cover mould screw fixed to wall plate.

timber skirting

wall plate bedded on d.p.c.

perimeter shuttering

horizontal noggin.

tilting fillet (optional)

polythene d.p.m taken up internal face of brickwork & tucked under d.p.c.

ground level

concrete base

1000g polythene d.p.m on expanded polystyrene insulation.

existing concrete base.

Detail 6.3 *Section of base built upon existing concrete base at ground level (1).*

bottom. This must be the easiest of all bases to construct and may be worth considering as an alternative to the standard concrete base shown in Detail 6.7 as it is easy enough to lay the initial slab if one doesn't already exist.

Detail 6.6 The removable base

Believe it or not the idea for this book originally came from the concept of a totally demountable workshop but, as with so many things, the concept changed with time and this more detailed construc-

49

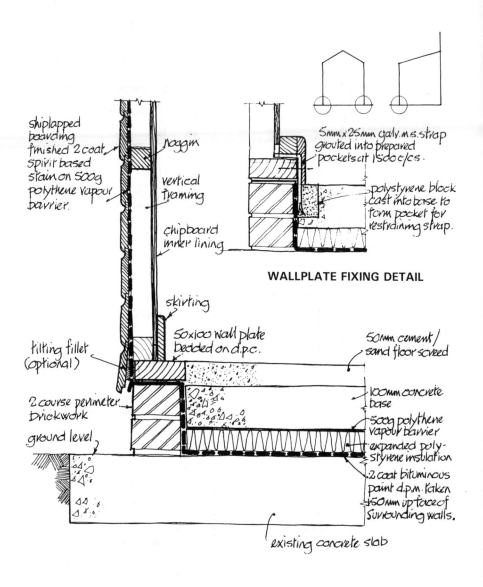

shiplapped boarding finished 2 coat spirit based stain on 500g polythene vapour barrier.

noggin

vertical framing

chipboard inner lining

WALLPLATE FIXING DETAIL

5mm x 25mm galv. m.s. strap grouted into prepared pockets at 1500 c/cs.

polystyrene block cast into base to form pocket for restraining strap.

skirting

tilting fillet (optional)

50 x 100 wall plate bedded on d.p.c.

2 course perimeter brickwork

ground level

50mm cement/ sand floor screed

100mm concrete base

500g polythene vapour barrier

expanded polystyrene insulation

2 coat bituminous paint d.p.m. taken 150mm up face of surrounding walls.

existing concrete slab

Detail 6.4 *Base built over existing concrete slab using bitumen-based paint-on sealer as DPM (2).*

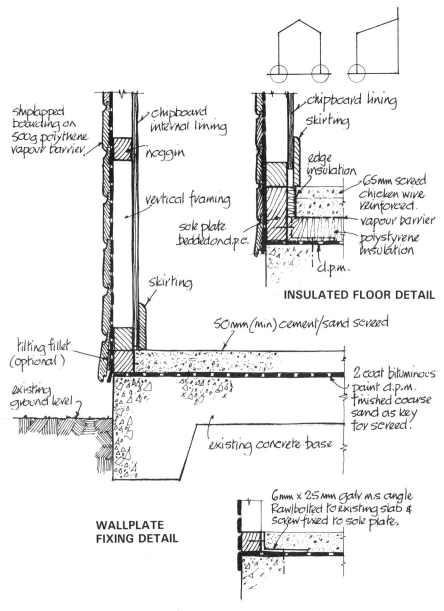

shiplapped boarding on 500g polythene vapour barrier.

chipboard internal lining

noggin

vertical framing

sole plate bedded on d.p.c.

skirting

chipboard lining

skirting

edge insulation

65mm screed chicken wire reinforced.

vapour barrier

polystyrene insulation

d.p.m.

INSULATED FLOOR DETAIL

tilting fillet (optional)

existing ground level

50mm (min) cement/sand screed

2 coat bituminous paint d.p.m. finished coarse sand as key for screed.

existing concrete base

6mm x 25mm galv. m.s angle Rawlbolted to existing slab & screw-fixed to sole plate.

WALLPLATE FIXING DETAIL

Detail 6.5 *Floor built over existing base which is above ground level (3).*

51

tion guide is the result. However, this is my pet floor – once completed it shares all the virtues and refinements of its permanent brothers but it can be dismantled and moved should you find it necessary to do so. "But who would do that?" I hear you say. I would contend that there are many people that might; anyone working on long term contracts, for instance, or Bank personnel who are often required to move to different branches every few years or so.

Anyway, enough justification, let's look at the design.

It has all of the elements of the other floors but they are modified to suit the need to move it at some time. Surrounding the whole floor is a ring of edging or kerb stones. They should be about 300mm deep and bevelled on the side to leave a flat top between 50–100mm wide depending on your choice of wall thickness. Cast your own if you wish – that way you can apply an external texture to them before they fully cure. The kerbing is set in a strip foundation of medium concrete with all the top edges laid dead level of course. Cut the end ones with a bolster chisel by going all around the outside with a chisel and hammer blows strong enough to mark the concrete where the break is to be. Once it's marked all the way round a couple of good blows with the chisel held vertical to the cut should shear it cleanly. It is best to lay them on a bed of sand to even out the stresses while belting them with the hammer. The same applies to the floor slabs. If you like pointing (filling in the joints) then mortar the joints between the kerbs. If not, don't worry about it and butt them tightly together as the DPM inside will stop any water from getting in.

Note the built-in attachment points for the walls. There are two ways of doing it: fit edging timbers as shown in other details

and then use a wide soleplate on the bottom of the wall to give a fixing, or build in galvanised metal cramps so they lock under the floorslabs as shown in Detail 6.6. One fixing point per 1.5m run will be fine so a 3m wall will require 3 fixings.

The hardcore should be really well compacted in this application because it truly supports the floor on top. Above this is the 'concrete', laid as dry mix and made as per old fashioned mortar; sand and lime mixed in a weak ratio of ten parts sand to one part lime. The mix should be only just moist – as per sandcastle sand – and it should be well tamped and level. Immediately after laying the sand/lime mix the slabs should be set on top and well tamped down to settle them. Spend extra time on getting them truly level with each other and use only dead flat slabs. When they are all down fill the spaces between them with a very dry and slightly stronger sand/lime mix of around 5:1. Brush the mix into the joints and ram it home until a good level surface is achieved. (Lime is nasty stuff – wear gloves at all times while handling it even when it's bagged up and wear a dust mask tp prevent dust inhalation.)

When the floor is finished try not to walk on it for at least a week and keep it covered for the first 48 hours. After that give it a sprinkling of water to really set the whole thing off. Just in case you're thinking about why the concrete has changed to a lime mix, it's because this type of mixture will separate easily and cleanly from the slabs and the remaining sub-base can be broken up very easily if necessary.

Detail 6.7 Standard concrete base
As the title says this is a standard concrete base design used generally by the building industry and adapted to suit our purpose and anticipated loading. My own base was

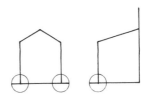

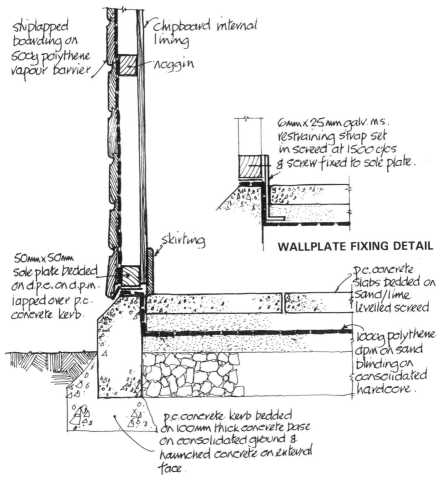

shiplapped
boarding on
500g polythene
vapour barrier

chipboard internal
lining

noggin

6mm x 25mm galv. m.s.
restraining strap set
in screed at 1500 c/cs
& screw-fixed to sole plate.

WALLPLATE FIXING DETAIL

skirting

50mm x 50mm
sole plate bedded
on d.p.c. on d.p.m.
lapped over p.c.
concrete kerb.

p.c. concrete
slabs bedded on
sand/lime
levelled screed

1000g polythene
dpm on sand
blinding on
consolidated
hardcore.

p.c. concrete kerb bedded
on 100mm thick concrete base
on consolidated ground &
haunched concrete on external
face.

Detail 6.6 *Section through removable floor.*

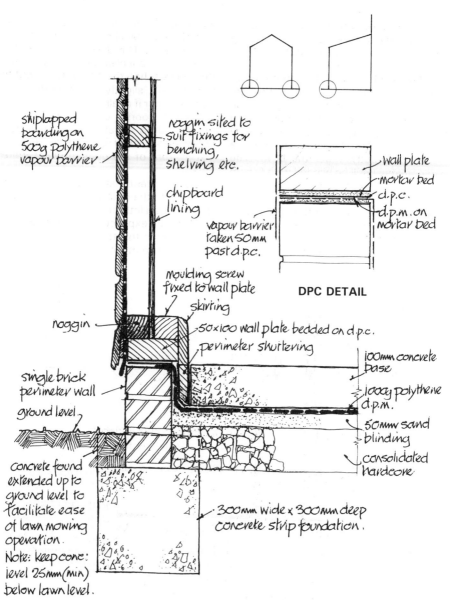

shiplapped
boarding on
500g polythene
vapour barrier

noggin sited to
suit fixings for
benching,
shelving etc.

chipboard
lining

vapour barrier
taken 50mm
past d.p.c.

DPC DETAIL

Wall plate
mortar bed
d.p.c.
d.p.m. on
mortar bed

moulding screw
fixed to wall plate

skirting

noggin

50x100 wall plate bedded on d.p.c.

perimeter shuttering

100mm concrete
base

1000g polythene
d.p.m.

50mm sand
blinding

consolidated
hardcore

single brick
perimeter wall

ground level

concrete found
extended up to
ground level to
facilitate ease
of lawn mowing
operation.
Note: keep conc.
level 25mm (min)
below lawn level.

300mm wide x 300mm deep
concrete strip foundation.

Detail 6.7 *Standard concrete base.*

54

built to this design and it is perfectly adequate for its use as an engineering workshop floor. The drawing shows brick perimeter walls although strip concrete could be used. I must admit that I prefer the brick-edged type because they are visible below the timber cladding and look much nicer than concrete strips. If you want to install a layer of insulation reduce the hardcore depth by 25mm and put the insulation directly under the DPM. The hardcore must still be blinded with 50mm of sand blinding so don't leave it out.

Detail 6.8 Base with lowered floor

This base is suitable for the infirm or wheelchair-bound people where the use of a ramp is not possible or suitable. It is a variation of the standard concrete base with the floor level set at, or just above, ground level. The design is straightforward enough but please note that the path that approaches the doorway should be sloped very slightly downwards away from the door if at all possible. In extreme cases the doorsill can be left out and replaced by a suitable wiper type door bottom seal backed up by a shallow gulley just in front of the door to direct water away.

It is important that the timber walls are still built on the brick perimeter walls and that causes a little complication in that the DPM will be exposed within the building. To overcome this there are two options. The first is to make the building walls as

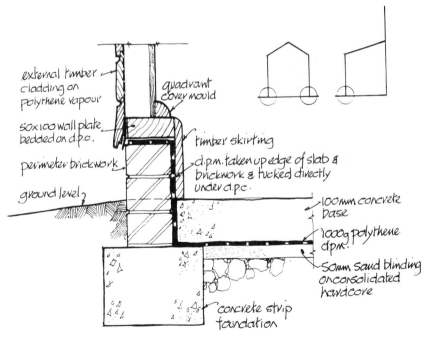

Detail 6.8 *Section through base with lowered floor.*

55

wide as the perimeter walls and then fit very deep (approx 200mm) skirting boards which will reach down to the floor level or, secondly with the 50mm walls, use a thick, and slightly wider, wall soleplate with a deep skirting screwed to the edge of it. Detail 6.8 shows sections through both arrangements.

Alternative floor finishes

All of the details of the concrete floors show a simple slab which doubles as both a structural member and the finished floor. However, some people are not going to be satisfied with that and will require either a really smooth fine grain floor surface or a wood feel under their feet.

Fine grain floor surface There are two ways to achieve this – paint on a chemical finish or lay a fine self-levelling screed. Modern chemical floor finishes are excellent, if expensive, and can provide a non-dusting impervious surface to work off. Laying a proper screed is equally as good but does involve yet more mixing, carrying and bending down. The screed should be

no less than 50mm deep and the concrete below it should be laid at a lower level to allow for this. Do not reduce the thickness of the concrete base as the screed doesn't add any structural strength to the floor at all. To make room for the 50mm screed reduce the hardcore depth. Remember what I said earlier about inserting an insulating layer under the screed and the need for a minimum thickness of 65mm with chicken wire reinforcement if this is done.

Where a screed is being laid over old concrete or on top of a DPM it is best not to use a polythene DPM but a bituminous one which has been sprinkled with dry sand while the bitumen is wet. This gives a good key for the screed and should prevent separation of the two floor stratas.

False wood floor In the section on timber floors I stated that there is a simpler and cheaper way of achieving the same end for those who would prefer a wood floor. The method shown in Detail 6.9 achieves this without all the costs or hassle of sawing joists and floorboards etc. I must agree with those people who say that

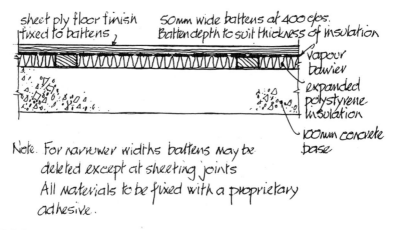

Note. For narrower widths battens may be deleted except at sheeting joints
All materials to be fixed with a proprietary adhesive.

Detail 6.9 *False wooden floor.*

56

timber floors are nice because they do have a spring in them – not measurable of course but it is perceived as a subtle give in the surface. The drawing is self-explanatory. All that I need to say is that the joints between the sheeting should be kept away from the aisle where you will walk if possible and that the whole lot – insulation and sheeting – can be stuck down if you prefer. The minimum thickness for the plywood should be 15mm but 20mm would be better. Obviously you should wait until the walls and roof are up before you lay it.

The text above and the information on the details should allow you to build a perfect base. When you've finished it will be time for a hot herbal bath – because believe me you'll need it! Then, once your blisters have healed up, you can start on the walls . . .

CHAPTER 7

The walls and roof

Don't know anything about carpentry? Join the club! I had a saw, a bag of screws and nails, a few tools and very little idea — yet my workshop looks fine. The reason for such a good result from such a poor outlook is the same one which makes two houses built from children's building blocks look exactly the same even when one is built by Mr. Average and the other by a Master Builder — it can only go together one way. Add to that any building's natural ability to absorb lots of errors without showing it and you're onto a winner. The design couldn't be any simpler with a double-skinned stud-type construction made up of a sheet inner skin and an interlocking weatherproof outer cladding fixed to a simple frame. Within the walls is a full vapour barrier and space for installing insulation. On top of the whole thing is a simple single skin roof — although more complicated versions are also given. It's all a piece of cake really!

So why not brick?
Someone somewhere is going to ask this question — so I'll answer it here: you could not be blamed for thinking that a far better and more rigid structure would be the result if bricks or building blocks were used instead of the design chosen. In

theory the stud wall could be replaced with a brick one but it would still have to be clad on one side or the other — depending on whether the bricks are on the outside or the inside — to produce a weatherproof structure because bricks are porous. Then there is the cost; bricks are very expensive and you need a lot to build even a small wall. They are also considerably heavier than stud walls so the foundations would have to be bigger to cope with the loading. Finally, bricks have a 'permanence' to them, and permanent structures involve bureaucrats — and we don't want any of those around do we?

Variants
In an attempt to prevent confusion this chapter describes only the details that relate to the construction of a free-standing, four-walled, workshop. That way the basic design does not become obscured by the details and text relating to the variants. See Chapter 8 for the design alterations needed to construct a lean-to version etc. You still need to read this chapter though because it contains the core information.

Material sizes
The minimum size for the frame members

should be 50mm × 25mm (with the 50mm producing the wall thickness) but the standard size for this design is 50mm × 50mm because the square section makes for easier corner construction and it is a readily available size. Detail 7.1 is included for those who want to use a 100mm wide wall and Details 7.10(c) and 7.11(c) show how to arrange the corner junctions. The same corner details will apply if you use 50mm × 25mm framing. I've already said that there is a large cost penalty for the 100mm size and that statement is based on the fact that you are unlikely to be able to obtain anything other that 100mm × 50mm timber. In fact 100mm × 25mm would be perfectly OK but, because it is really a plank, you probably won't get it in rough sawn timber.

The following table gives the relative sizes of the framing, inner skin and frame spacings but note that the 12mm inner lining thickness will only be suitable for light duties and it should be increased to 15mm or more if it is to take high shelf or bench loadings.

WALL MATERIAL SIZES

Frame Sizes mm	Frame Spacing mm	Inner Lining mm	Cladding mm
50 × 25	300	15	12
50 × 50	400	12	12
50 × 50	600	15	12
75 × 50	600	15	12
100 × 25	600	15	12

Although I have given the frame spacings they should only be used as a guide. Set the actual spacing as close as you can to these but take into account where the inner skin joints will be or you may have to put in additional verticals to provide a fixing. The outer cladding should be at least 12mm thick and (preferably) of 150mm deep planks. The wallplates and toprails should be around 50mm thick with a width to match either the DPC (at the bottom) or the wall (at the top) as applicable.

The size of the rafters is dependent on the span and, at least in the UK, need only to be strong enough to support their own and the roof sheeting weight without sagging. This translates into some pretty spindly rafter sizes – but it must always be remembered that the roof will not stand a man's weight. In more northerly climes the roof will have to contend with a full winter's accumulation of snow and could end up having to support a considerable weight – so I would suggest that you only build a pitched roof with a pitch angle of at least 45 degrees to shed the stuff. If you can only construct a mono-pitch roof then you must at least double the figures given in the table.

The roof design allows for a sheet covering which is then covered in a waterproof material. It will not withstand the loading from any type of conventional roof tiles. If you want something a little more decorative then you could use American-style wood shingles, contoured and coloured metal decorative roofing panels (once known as corrugated iron sheets) or throw up (builder's term meaning erect upwards) a false roof panel with a few rows of tiles attached with the proper roof hidden behind it.

The walls
The walls are just spacers between the floor and the roof so the details of the lower ends are shown in the previous chapter in Details 6.1 to 6.8. The details relating to workshops with brick perimeter walls all show framing widths of 50mm as previously explained. The offset of the wall towards the outer edge of the

ROOF MATERIAL SIZES

Roof Type	Span m	Rafter W × D mm	Rafter Spacing mm	Sheeting Thickness mm
Detail 7.2/3/4	2	25 × 50	400	6
Detail 7.2/3/4	3	25 × 75	300	12
Detail 7.5	2	25 × 50	600	6
Detail 7.5	3	38 × 75	400	6

perimeter wall is very important so don't be tempted to line up the inside of the wall with the inside of the base and skip the overlap as a considerable amount of water could find its way under the floor and make it unstable. Where the base perimeter wall has been cast, or edging stones have been used, this problem will not arise because you would design the widths to match up − *wouldn't you?*

The tops of the walls vary slightly according to the roof type being fitted. There are four roof types as shown in Details 7.2 to 7.5 and they also show how the top of the wall should be constructed for each type. Detail 7.7 shows a vertical cross-section through the door opening and includes both inward and outward opening doors. Just to make sure that you have enough information to install the door frame correctly Details 7.8 and 7.9 show plan sections through the door frame for both types.

The other two significant details show how to make the wall junctions − or corners to those that don't understand building jargon! Detail 7.10 is a section through the corner showing the frame doubling needed to provide a fixing for the inner skin together with the simple overlap method of finishing the outer cladding. Detail 7.11 shows the same corner but with the cladding joint finished (more professionally) with a corner strip. Each detail has three parts: (a) is for a corner where there is only one upright, (b) is for a corner which has been made up from two frames screwed together (so there are two uprights) and (c) is for a corner where the framing is of unequal dimensions, such as 75mm × 50mm.

The roof types

Detail 7.2 is the simplest possible but its use is dependent on the weatherproofing being the 'paint-on' liquid rubber type or a welded butyl sheeting as it cannot be felted very satisfactorily. Detail 7.3 shows a mono-pitch felted roof, similar to the previous detail but this time with all of the additional bits to allow it to be covered with mineral felt. Detail 7.4 is another felted roof but this time designed with a ventilated cavity so that a full ceiling can be fitted. Detail 7.5 shows a simple, felted, pitched roof. While the last three are shown with mineral felt covering they could equally be painted or even fitted with a butyl sheet covering.

In the previous chapter I said that the worst thing that you can do with wood is to seal it up. The same situation as the timber floors occurs again with the roof. The problem this time lies with the ceiling because if one is fitted to the thin roof sections proposed here, then the cavity becomes sealed and a serious problem is in the making, hence the addition of Detail 7.4 for a ventilated roof. All 'full-size' roofs are ventilated, including flat ones, but it is not easy to do − particularly on the skinny thing that I am suggesting. For

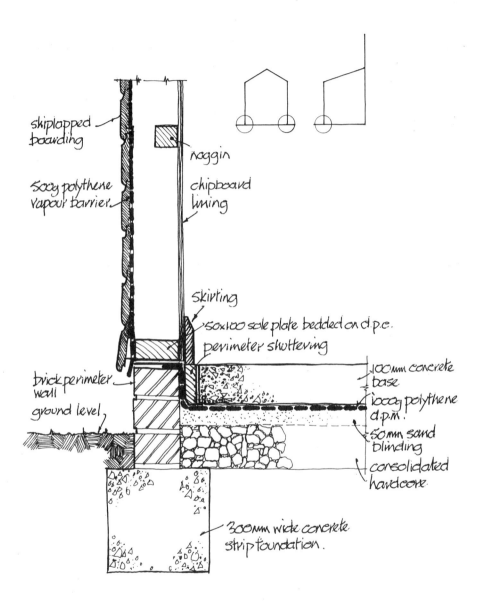

skiplapped boarding

Sooy polythene vapour barrier

briick perimeter wall

ground level

naggin

chipboard lining

Skirting

50x100 sole plate bedded on d.p.c.
perimeter shuttering

100mm concrete base

1000g polythene d.p.m.

50mm sand blinding

consolidated hardcore

300mm wide concrete strip foundation.

Detail 7.1 *Detail of base using 50mm × 100mm framing.*

61

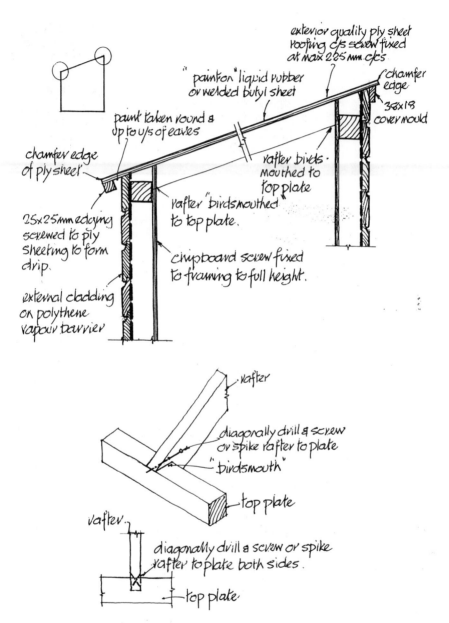

exterior quality ply sheet
roofing c/s screw fixed
at max 225 mm c/cs

"paint on" liquid rubber
or welded butyl sheet

chamfer
edge

38x18
cover mould

paint taken round 8
up to u/s of eaves

chamfer edge
of ply sheet

rafter birds·
mouthed to
top plate

25x25mm edging
screwed to ply
sheeting to form
drip.

rafter "birdsmouthed
to top plate.

chipboard screw fixed
to framing to full height.

external cladding
on polythene
vapour barrier

rafter

diagonally drill 8 screw
or spike rafter to plate

"birdsmouth"

top plate

rafter.

diagonally drill 8 screw or spike
rafter to plate both sides.

top plate.

Detail 7.2 *Section through simple mono-pitched roof.*

62

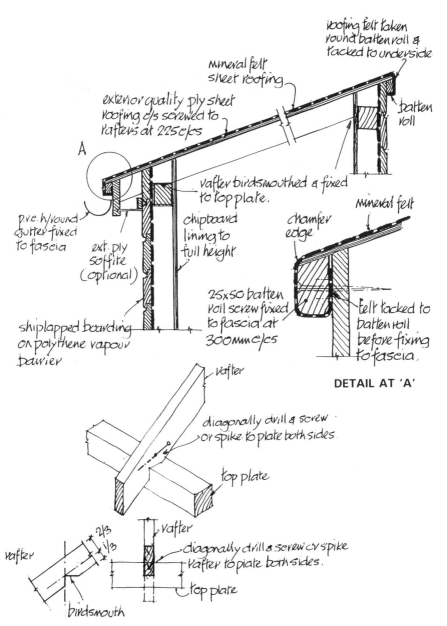

roofing felt taken round batten roll & tacked to underside

mineral felt sheet roofing

exterior quality ply sheet roofing c/s screwed to rafters at 225 c/cs

batten roll

A

rafter birdsmouthed & fixed to top plate.

mineral felt

p.v.c. h/round gutter fixed to fascia

ext. ply soffite (optional)

chipboard lining to full height

chamfer edge

shiplapped boarding on polythene vapour barrier

25x50 batten roll screw fixed to fascia at 300mm c/cs

felt tacked to batten roll before fixing to fascia.

DETAIL AT 'A'

rafter

diagonally drill & screw or spike to plate both sides

top plate

2/3
1/3

rafter

vafter

diagonally drill & screw or spike rafter to plate both sides.

top plate

birdsmouth

Detail 7.3 *Section through felted mono-pitched roof.*

63

this reason my own roof does not have a ceiling but what I have done instead is to wedge close-fitting insulation panels the same depth as the rafters over the whole roof and painted over it. The result is really quite acceptable.

If you want a ceiling but not the complexity involved in providing the ventilation, you could still fit ceiling panels but with a gap of 25mm left open at the ends to allow air to circulate between the rafters. Note that roofs fitted with a ceiling need the first and last rafters to be doubled up to provide a fixing for the ceiling panels as the end ones are built within the

thickness of the wall frame. To insulate such a roof you can still fit close fitting polystyrene sheets between the rafters but only make them half the depth of the rafters and push them tightly up against the roof panel.

If your workshop is going to be in the 2.2–3m span range then seriously consider a pitched roof as shown in Detail 7.5. There is something nice about a well proportioned gable end (the pointed bit) as against the rather perfunctory look of a mono-pitch roof. It is also well worth considering if you want a fully insulated roof with a ceiling because it is easier to

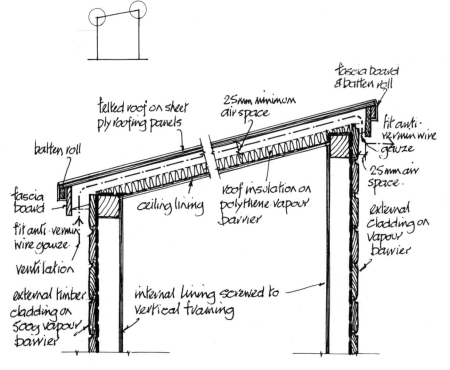

Detail 7.4 *Section through lean-to ventilated roof.*

64

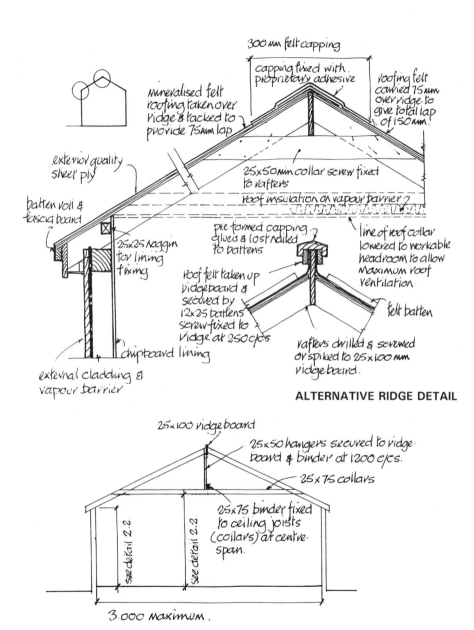

300 mm felt capping

capping fixed with proprietary adhesive

roofing felt carried 75 mm over ridge to give total lap of 150 mm

mineralised felt roofing taken over ridge & tacked to provide 75 mm lap

exterior quality sheet ply

25 x 50 mm collar screw fixed to rafters

roof insulation on vapour barrier ?

batten roll & fascia board

25 x 25 noggin for lining fixing

pre-formed capping glued & lost nailed to battens

line of roof collar lowered to workable headroom to allow maximum roof ventilation

roof felt taken up ridgeboard & secured by 12 x 25 battens screw-fixed to ridge at 250 c/cs

felt batten

chipboard lining

rafters drilled & screwed or spiked to 25 x 100 mm ridge board.

external cladding & vapour barrier

ALTERNATIVE RIDGE DETAIL

25 x 100 ridgeboard

25 x 50 hangers secured to ridge board & binder at 1200 c/cs.

25 x 75 collars

25 x 75 binder fixed to ceiling joists (collars) at centre span.

see detail 2.2

see detail 2.2

3.000 maximum.

Detail 7.5 *Felted pitched roof.*

65

build than the ventilated mono-pitch type. All that has to be done to provide for the insulation is to set the collars at a suitable height, install some mid-span hangers, sheet out the underside and place the insulation. The only proviso is that the upper roof section *must* then be ventilated by means of at least two little ventilators fitted in each of the gable ends. Alternatively the space above the collars could be used for storage of long items – but fit the hangers as the basic collar design is only sized for absorbing the roof thrust.

Construction notes

I stated at the beginning of this chapter that my carpentry skills are slight! However, in the end this 'skill shortfall' did not matter but there was a point in the construction where it showed. I'm referring to the stage where the framing for all

of the walls and roof was complete but no lining out or cladding was fixed. In a 'normal' situation the following stages would be:

(1) Sheet the roof
(2) Fix the vapour barrier
(3) Fix exterior cladding
(4) Fit wall insulation
(5) Fix internal lining

The problem was that my rickety pile of sticks would never have withstood the belting that nailing the external cladding on would have subjected it to. My sequence was a little different:

(1) Sheet the roof – with screws
(2) Fix internal lining – with screws
(3) Fit wall insulation – I didn't install insulation but if I had it would have been here

This is actually my shed but the same method of construction was used. Note the perimeter walls and the fact that the framing sits right on the outer edge of them. (The framing on the shed is only 25mm square so it looks very spindly.)

(4) Fix vapour barrier – with staples

(5) Fix external cladding – with nails

By the time I started nailing the cladding on the structure was nice and rigid. You can follow whatever route that you choose but obviously it is best to try and get the roof on at the earliest opportunity, especially in Britain. If it's pouring with rain some degree of weatherproofing can be achieved by fixing the vapour barrier in place at the outset, including over the roof area as a temporary measure.

The rest of this chapter is made up of notes relevant to each part of the construction sequence but before you pick up your saw and start laying into the woodpile just ponder these very true words first – *measure twice, cut once!* It might stop you ending up with a pile of offcuts that's bigger than your workshop!

Framing out

Probably the easiest way of erecting the whole thing is to build the frame directly off the base and that is what most constructors will do. It is easy because you can 'cut to fit' whereas offsite constr- uction requires quite good control over the dimensions to ensure that it will all go together. The only real problem occurs if it rains. The answer, as I said earlier, is to get the rudimentary frame up, staple the vapour barrier in position and then work inside. If you put it over the rafters as well remove it as the roof sheeting is put on.

The first thing to do is to cut the wall- plates so that they are flush with, or very slightly overlap, the outer edge of the base while at the same time keeping the inside lengths equal to half multiples of the inner sheet width (or slightly greater). If you followed the planning as per Chapter 2 you will already have set the base dimen- sions to allow for this. Then use the wall- plates as the basis for construction and

erect the verticals and cross ties on them. If the frames are pre-built as simple rectangles there will already be a horizontal 50mm wide member fixed on top of the wallplate. If the frame is built directly off the wallplate you will have to insert noggins between the verticals to provide a fixing for the inner sheeting. All that is needed is a simple frame built up from the base which is then stiffened by the addition of the sheeting. The finished frame should have subframes built in for the windows and door frame to be attached. The most difficult part is getting the first corner set up. I did it by pre- building the side and front framing as simple rectangles and they were lifted up and set vertical and square to one other. With these two skeletal frames up it was easy to build from them. Alternatively the door frame could be propped in position and the rest built off it.

As for joining the frame members you are spoilt for choice and Detail 7.6 shows three ways of doing it. The easiest method of all is by 'spiking' or cross nailing the ends of the verticals into the horizontal rails as shown but do drill pilot holes in the vertical timbers to prevent splitting. The next easiest method is to use proprietary 90-degree brackets fixed by short screws, and the last is by fitting spacers or 'noggins' between the verticals and either nailing or screwing the frame members to them. *It has to be said that using screws for the joints is the best way of joining the timbers, both for strength and initial stress.* The carpenters amongst you will of course ignore all of this heresy and spend hours lovingly chiselling out perfect tenon joints or holes for dowels etc., but those with the same skills in carpentry as I have needn't worry as the importance of the frame joints diminishes drastically when the sheeting is erected.

Where the inner skin panels butt to-

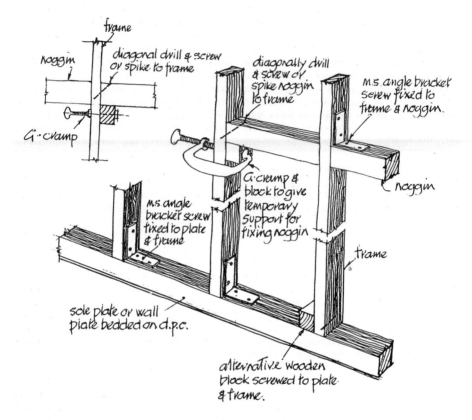

frame

noggin

diagonal drill & screw or spike to frame

G-cramp

diagonally drill & screw or spike noggin to frame

m.s. angle bracket screw fixed to frame & noggin.

noggin

m.s. angle bracket screw fixed to plate & frame

G-cramp & block to give temporary support for fixing noggin

frame

sole plate or wall plate bedded on d.p.c.

alternative wooden block screwed to plate & frame.

Detail 7.6 *Frame jointing methods.*

gether, the verticals that they will be screwed onto should either be doubled up or wider than the other ones to give an adequate fixing to both sheets. Similarly, in the corners, extra verticals are necessary to provide a fixing for the end of one of the sheets as shown in Details 7.10 and 11. Three variations are shown – the top one for single uprights (on site framing), the middle one for twin uprights (pre-built frames) and the lower one for unequal

framing (such as 100 × 50mm). While you are on the framing, build in extra horizontal noggins to use as reinforcements for benches or heavy cupboard fixings as the high density chipboard lining will hold screws for reasonable loads, such as ordinary shelving, but it cannot be expected to take concentrated ones. *Don't forget to mark all of the vertical frame members centrelines on the floor and toprail because you'll need to know*

68

where they are when you come to drill the screw holes through the inner sheeting.

The wallplate at the bottom of the wall should be the same width as the top of the perimeter wall regardless of the stud wall thickness in order to clamp the DPC. On a 100mm wide wall this automatically happens but, where the studwork is less than this, a separate wallplate is screwed onto the bottom of the frame as shown in the Details in Chapter 6. The simplest way to fix the wall to the base is to drill through the wallplate into the base and use plastic plugs and brass screws spaced about 1 − 1.5m apart but, as this involves drilling through the DPC, there's a slight possibility that in areas with very wet ground conditions water could find its way up into the framing. If you think that this is likely, squirt a dollop of silicone type sealer down the holes before inserting the plastic plugs and avoid using wood plugs or steel screws. I fixed my walls down in this way but if you look at the Details you will see that Peter has also shown various cramps as another method of holding them down as well.

Windows and door

Although the window and door frames should be built into the framing the wallplate should not pass under the sill (unless you want a higher step for some reason) but the DPC must. To fix the door and windows I simply wedged them in position in the studwork, framed around and then screwed them in place. If 'full-size' window and door frames are being used in a narrow wall, some juggling will have to be done to spread the excess depth so that it isn't obvious. Needless to say the inside face of the frames should be set so that they will be at least flush with the face of the inner skin when that is fitted. What is very important is that neither frames are

recessed into the outer cladding as it will be difficult to seal them to the cladding later. I set mine so that they would end up just proud of the outer cladding by about 3mm. Details 7.7 to 7.9 show how to arrange the door for inward and outward opening but they only really apply if you construct the door frame yourself.

The window frames don't require any fitting instructions because they simply slot into the framing with the windowsill sticking proud of the cladding.

Prefabricated walls

If you like setting out dimensions, (or prefer to build as much as possible on a nice dry garage floor), you could construct the walls almost completely away from the base. I say almost because to my mind it would be better to build the frames, inner skin and window frames etc. on the garage floor, but to fix the outer cladding only when they are fixed to the base. I know that this will rather defeat the object of prefabrication but it will be a lot easier to line up the cladding at the corners and it will probably be a far better job. If, however, you decide to build the *complete* walls for erection later remember that the holding down screws are *inside* the wall thickness so either leave off a strip of the inner skin at the bottom or use built-in cramps as for the demountable version as per Detail 6.6. Fixing the cladding only after the walls are erected also applies to the demountable version, although it won't have to be done that way again when it is moved. The good point about prefabricating the walls is that all the inner sheeting can be cut to size and the individual frame members screwed to it − rather than the other way round.

Insulation

By far the best sort of insulation is the sheet polystyrene sold specifically for this

69

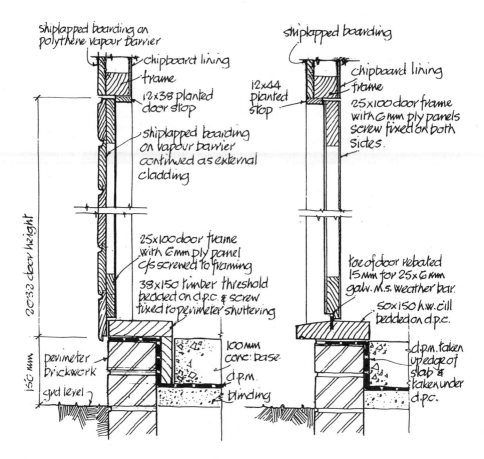

Detail 7.7 *Vertical sections of inward and outward opening doors.*

purpose. The sheets can be cut very easily with a craft knife and they can be made a nice snug fit between the framing. The sheets are available in various thicknesses and you should select a size that fills the available gap. Alternatively there is a compacted form of roof insulation – rock fibre in sheets – and they too can be cut quite easily but with a saw this time. Always fit the insulation at the last minute before panelling it in and avoid getting it wet. The water won't actually harm the insulation but you don't want to seal dampness into the wall if at all possible.

One of the best natural insulants is – still air – so I didn't bother! The point to stress though is that it must be still. If the gap is over about 75mm eddy currents will begin to circulate and heat loss will start to occur.

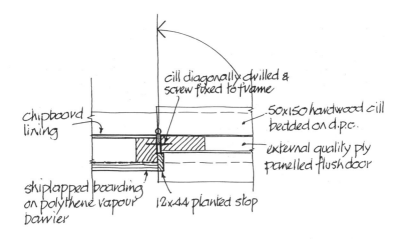

Detail 7.8 *Inward opening door.*

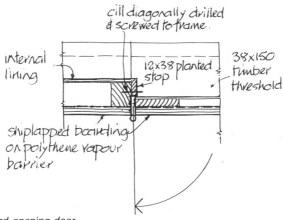

Detail 7.9 *Outward opening door.*

Vapour barrier

An essential part of the building fabric is the vapour barrier. Details 6.1 to 6.7 and 7.2 and 7.5 show how it must be built into the walls so that it interleaves correctly with both the roof and the base DPM. The idea is that if water is poured over the outside of the membrane it will always be directed away from the building interior. If you are working in dry weather leave it off until just before fixing the outer cladding to minimise the chance of

71

The shed again, this time showing the weatherboarding cladding overlapping the perimeter walls. The waterbutt shown here is a temporary one and there's the cat! How do they know that fresh concrete is about?

damage. Use a staple gun or thumbtacks to fix it in place but be very careful not to tear it. Where overlaps occur make them at least 150mm wide. Initially, cover the whole of the walls with it including the door and window openings and then make diagonal cuts in the openings so that the membrane can be pressed back against the framing. Don't cut away the excess until the outer cladding is fixed in place.

If the walls are insulated the vapour barrier should (technically) be repeated on both sides of the stud wall framing. By all means do this if you wish because the material is cheap enough, but as the walls are relatively thin and no air movement is possible I would not fit the inner barrier. (Please note that the reverse is true when lining out an existing brick wall and the gap is insulated – the barrier should be immediately behind the inner lining and covering the insulation.)

The roof

As the frame goes up there comes a point where the rafters have to be set out. Details 7.2 to 7.5 show the four roof designs and the way that the rafters should be fitted and I would suggest that you study these very carefully. This is the only position where something bordering decent carpentry is required as the ends of the rafters have to be birdsmouthed so they sit nicely on top of the toprail. Just to make it worse, all of the rafters must be cut the same or the finished roof will be rippled where it is fixed to the uneven rafters. The only way that I found of doing this was to mark the shape to be removed on all three of the rafter faces affected and to then chisel out the unwanted material. The marking out can be made easy by folding a piece of card to fit round the three faces after shaping it with scissors. That way all of the cut-outs will be the same. Alternatively, you can cramp all of the rafters together and chop out the unwanted material as if it were one big rafter. Either way the result should be reasonable. If you do mess up you can slice layers of plywood and use them as shims.

Starting with the mono-pitch jobs first. The simple roof is a little different to the felted version in that the rafters do not overshoot the walls so they just need the ends to be cut to an acute angle. You are aiming for the end of the rafter to be set at exactly the front edge of the toprail so there won't be a gap under the roof sheeting when it's fitted. Don't worry too much about this point because the cladding, which will be fitted later, will be pushed up against the underside of the roof as Detail 7.2 shows anyway. Detail 7.3 shows the correct proportions for the birdsmouth cut-out on the felted roof rafters – get it wrong and the roof eaves could sag because of rafter end failure. The ventilated roof looks a bit complicated in comparison to the other types, although the lean-to version is even worse (see Chapter 8) but all the bits are necessary I can assure you. The idea is to get a free passage of air, but not rain, both into and out of the roof space. This translates into providing a downward facing slot at the front and rear of the roof and placed so that even in the worst weather rain will not be driven in.

Whichever mono-pitch you are building the procedure is the same: fix the end rafters with their outer faces flush with the outside edge of the wall framing and then space the intermediate ones equally along the length. When they are all ready,

spike or screw them onto the wall toprails. Regardless of whether the roof is single slope or pitched the frame members in the end walls should run right up to meet the rafters, that way you have something to nail the cladding onto. Finally, work out whether there will be any joins in your roof sheeting at 90 degrees to the rafters and fit noggins between them so that the joint edges will be supported. In truth, 'across slope' joins in the roof sheeting on the simple painted roof is not a good idea – it is better to waste a little material and only have 'down slope' butt joints.

Pitched roofs are normally made up from pre-assembled units called trusses which can be purchased surprisingly cheaply – cheaper in fact than you would have to pay for the timber alone. However, with the sort of spans that we are working with it is unlikely that any are available commercially – so you will have to make them (although in our roof they will be built on the job). Build the end, or gable, walls without any intermediate verticals and with the wall top timbers sloping up as rafters, terminating at the ridge board. Then build in the rest of the rafters by spiking them to the eaves walls toprails and to the ridgeboard at even spacings. You can then build in the gable wall verticals so that they run right up to the underside of the end rafters. Finally, *and really importantly*, screw the collars in the lowest possible position taking into account the headroom that you need *before you load the roof. The collars are very important and must not be omitted as they triangulate the roof elements and stop the loaded roof from pushing the eaves walls away from each other.* An alternative construction would be to build the walls as per a completely flat roof and build little gables on top of them at each end. If you intend to fit a ceiling or use the collars as a material rack don't forget to install the hangers which tie the collars to the ridgeboard and stiffen up the whole assembly as shown in the detail. For what it costs in terms of the timber used I would fit hangers anyway — you might load the collars up later and forget all about this little necessity — although probably not for long!

Sheeting the roof

While it is best to try to avoid joins in the roof sheeting on the simple roof, it is OK on the other types. Don't go mad though and start fixing in little panels all butted together just to save on the cost of another sheet. Cut the first sheet, not forgetting to allow for the eaves overhang of around 75mm, lay it on the roof and mark its edges on the rafters and noggins with a pencil. At the same time mark all the centrelines of the rafters onto the sheet for the fixing screws later. Remove the sheet and run a 3mm bead of non-setting sealant onto the rafters and noggins all around the edges (this can be omitted on the felted versions). Reposition the sheet and fix it in place with just a couple of panel pins — just enough to hold it — then drill all of the screw holes spaced at around 150mm apart with a short or stopped drill and screw it down tight with brass screws. Cut the next sheet and repeat the procedure ensuring that the sealant is forced out of the joint between the sheets. Repeat until the whole roof is sheeted over making sure that you don't forget to wipe the surplus sealant off the joints with a damp cloth. To finish off the simple painted version tack on a strip of wood to form the 'drip' and cut and fit the various eaves panels etc. as shown in the details for the other types.

It is especially important on the painted roof version that the sheets are screwed down because the panels must never move or the seal may be stressed and broken. Nailed panels move in response to climatic changes and the nails eventually loosen. Anyway, plywood does not take kindly to being nailed and, as the skinny design put forward here relies on the beam effect for its strength, I would only use screws.

Covering the roof

There are three choices of covering: painted rubber, mineral felt and butyl sheeting.

Painted rubber There are several types of this finish which is sold not only for roofing purposes but also for sealing concrete fishponds. They are essentially a liquid rubber formulation which, although water based, dries to an impervious rubber sheet. My own workshop roof is covered this way and after 10 years has shown no signs of failure or deterioration. Visit your local DIY centre or builders' merchant and take your pick. When painting this material onto the simple roof be sure to paint under the eaves and right up to the cladding. There are only two pieces of advice that I can offer; first, follow the instructions to the letter including, if necessary, painting on an undercoat. Secondly, cover the sheeting joints with a scrim set into the wet solution and then paint over again when the first coat is dry. This second item is very important as the only point of weakness in the whole roof is the joint between the panels. Scrim is a 50mm wide strip of reinforcing tape made of fibreglass or any *manmade* fibre such as nylon. (Note — If the instructions on the tin suggest that the roof timber can be cheap chipboard, don't believe it. I had to rip the whole roof off a shed after falling for that one!)

Mineral felt This is bought in rolls from any DIY shop or builders' merchant. It must be fitted correctly for it to have a reasonable life – and I would work on the basis that it will be about 10 years. To install it look closely at Details 7.3 to 7.5 and 7.12 and proceed as follows:

(a) Cut the felt into strips as long as the roof plus about 300mm for the mono-pitch roof and plain pitched roof. Note that the seams must run down the slope and not along it, and cut sufficient strips to cover the roof once with overlaps between adjoining strips of 150mm. (You can put as many layers on as you like but one should be sufficient.)

(b) Lay the strips across the roof for a couple of hours to allow the felt to uncurl, warm up, and stretch.

(c) Fold back 50mm of one end of each strip with the inside of the felt inside the fold.

(d) Facing the workshop on the low side of the roof and with the inside of the felt facing you, tack the folded end level with the top of the fascia board with a couple of tacks. On the ends of the roof leave an overlap of 100mm over the edge of the roof. Repeat the tacking up process until all of the felting is up. You should now have all of the strips hanging from the fascia with the inside of the felt facing you.

(e) Nail or screw a batten along the full length of the fascia with its top edge in line with the roof so that it traps all of the folded felt underneath.

(f) On the high side of the roof nail another batten with its top edge level with the roof.

(g) Gently fold each strip of felt over the roof so that it rolls round the batten, goes up the roof and hangs down the back. Pull all of the strips as tight as you can.

(h) Pulling the felt as tight as possible,

fold it round the batten and tack it with short tacks on the underneath of the batten.

(i) This is the difficult bit. The correct way to deal with the sides, or verges, is to neatly tuck and fold the felt over the verge and screw a batten along the edge with the felt trapped underneath, then trim off the surplus all round. You will quickly find that felt doesn't like being 'tucked and folded' so here's the easier, alternative, method: cut the felt down the slope exactly in line with the edge of the roof and screw a batten down to fix it in position. Close the edge of the roof with another batten to make it look tidy. Detail 7.12 shows the method.

(j) Cut battens for each felt sheet overlap on the roof slope and, using galvanised or brass round head screws, screw them down tight along the seam so that they run down the slope.

(k) Wait until it rains!

The procedure for covering the pitched roofs varies slightly to the above but the version with the ridgeboard flush with the roofing sheets needs no explanation as it is obvious from the drawing. However, the pitched roof with exposed ridgeboard does need the differences with the description above explained. In this case cut the felt strips about 200mm longer than needed and replace steps (g) and (h) with the following:

(g) Pull the sheets gently over the eaves batten and up the slope until they are pulled tightly over the ridgeboard. Tap in a few tacks to hold the sheets in place and fit the holding battens as shown. Trim off any surplus to leave approximately 25mm sticking up above the ridgeboard. Repeat on the other side.

(h) Fold the surplus over each other and over the ridgeboard tightly. Then fix your choice of timber capping onto the ridgeboard taking great care not to damage or overtension the felt.

Butyl sheeting This must be just about the best roof material available and is well worth finding a supplier and getting a price for your roof. It is ideally suited to a flat simple roof which is not linked to another wall – although this too can be accommodated. The pre-formed shape is made by specialist companies to dimensions supplied by the purchaser and is made slightly small so it stretches during fitting. Return edges are welded in and these are tacked down round the sides on installation. Even the simple pitched roof shape would not be a problem for this material.

Whichever roofing material you choose it will almost certainly be black or dark grey which, as we all know, are colours that soak up heat from the sun at an incredible rate. The result can be an unbearably hot workshop which hardly cools down at night because the whole fabric of the building radiates back the vast amount of energy that was collected during the day. If you have this problem there are special silver and white paints available for treating roofs and they are very effective at reflecting the heat away.

Internal lining

To fit the inner sheeting, cut the width as accurately as possible and, if there are to be any gaps, arrange for them to be in the corners where it is easy to fill them in later before decorating. Don't worry too much about the height because any shortfall can be lost behind a skirting board. Prop a panel in place with the short end of the rocking wedge (Detail 4.2) under it at mid-span and push down on the other end of the wedge to force the sheet against the roof. If you haven't made a rocking wedge use rough timber wedges knocked in at the bottom to force the sheet up. Then, using the marks on the floor as centreline guides, drill screw holes through the panels every 150mm onto every frame member and screw in place with number 6 screws. With 12mm panels use 25mm screws and for 15mm panels use 25mm ones. Now you see why I suggested getting hold of an electric screwdriver! Set the torque so that the screw heads are pulled in flush with the panel face.

External cladding

Cladding is very easy to fit and the method is obvious so, providing you set the bottom ones dead level and overhanging the base to give the weatherboard effect, the rest is easy. Well, not quite – what happens at the corners?

The way an ordinary garden shed is clad is one way of dealing with the corners as shown in Detail 7.10. The short sides are clad so that the planks are cut dead width to the sides. The front and back walls are then planked so that the ends mask the exposed ends of the side cladding. This still leaves the ends of the planks on the two long sides exposed of course but they are round the sides – if you see what I mean! It's not really a good idea to leave the end grain of any wood directly exposed to the elements and there is another way of dealing with the corners which solves this problem.

The alternative method hides the end grain of the cladding by providing a corner strip which the cladding abuts as shown in Detail 7.11. It also looks a lot better than the other method. First, clad the front and rear walls only so that the ends of the planks are exactly the length of the walls. Then cut four lengths of 15 × 38mm

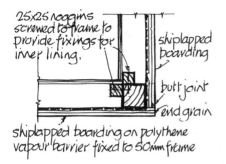

25x25 noggins screwed to frame to provide fixings for inner lining.

shiplapped boarding

butt joint

end grain

shiplapped boarding on polythene vapour barrier fixed to 50mm frame

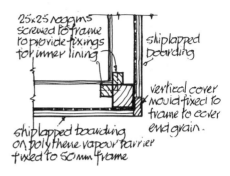

25x25 noggins screwed to frame to provide fixings for inner lining

shiplapped boarding

vertical cover mould fixed to frame to cover end grain.

shiplapped boarding on polythene vapour barrier fixed to 50mm frame

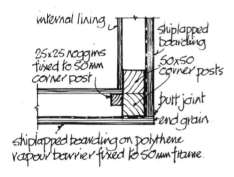

internal lining

shiplapped boarding

25x25 noggins fixed to 50mm corner post

50x50 corner posts

butt joint

end grain

shiplapped boarding on polythene vapour barrier fixed to 50mm frame.

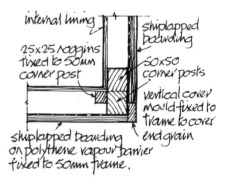

internal lining

shiplapped boarding

25x25 noggins fixed to 50mm corner post

50x50 corner posts

vertical cover mould fixed to frame to cover end grain

shiplapped boarding on polythene vapour barrier fixed to 50mm frame.

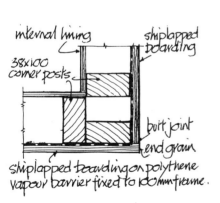

internal lining

shiplapped boarding

38x100 corner posts

butt joint

end grain

shiplapped boarding on polythene vapour barrier fixed to 100mm frame.

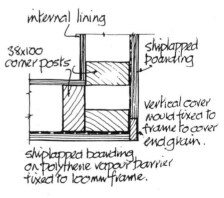

internal lining

shiplapped boarding

38x100 corner posts

vertical cover mould fixed to frame to cover end grain.

shiplapped boarding on polythene vapour barrier fixed to 100mm frame.

Detail 7.10
Plan of plain corner wall junction.

Detail 7.11
Plan of capped corner wall junction.

77

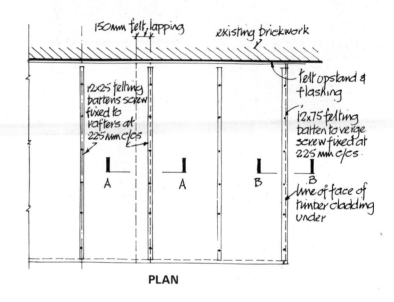

PLAN

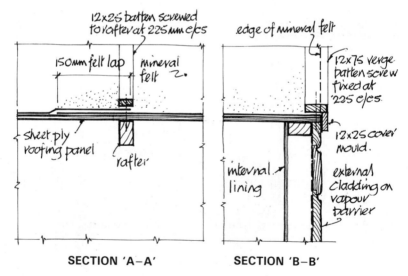

SECTION 'A–A'   **SECTION 'B–B'**

Detail 7.12 *Felt roof details.*

78

Back to the workshop. Here you can see the vapour barrier and the cladding as well as the extension in the foreground which is a covered drying area.

Finished and stained. The door is at the far end. Here's proof that photographs lie — the building looks extremely small because of the angle of the picture and the vertical surroundings.

A view along the face of the cladding showing the neat finish to the corner when a batten is used. This picture also shows the drying area floor which later became the extension.

batten to the eaves to weatherboard dimension and nail them vertically on the corner so that the ends of the exposed planks are covered. Finally, clad the end walls with planks cut to the dimension between the battens. If ply sheeting is being used, either follow the instructions above, or overlap the edges on the corners as per the shed example and then fix a batten over the exposed end grain on each corner.

The details show the bottom cladding plank set out at the lowest edge by a 'tilting fillet'. This does just what its name implies and it looks quite good too. It is

optional but only where the corner batten described above is fitted – otherwise the splay opens up a gap on the corners.

How you fix the cladding depends on which stage of construction it is fitted. If it goes up before the internal lining then I would suggest you screw it on with galvanised or plated screws. If it goes on right at the end then nail it on by 'splay nailing' using only galvanised nails. 'Splay nailing' means that the top nails point slightly upwards and the lower ones slightly downwards and it really secures the planks, preventing them from twisting or pulling away slightly when the wood dries right out in high summer. Be careful to get it right as this way of fixing the planks can make it very difficult to get them off again later if you have to.

When cladding round the window and door openings pull the vapour barrier out between the frame and the plank ends and trim off the excess flush with the cladding. To make it really weatherproof squirt a bead of non-setting sealant into the planking/frame joint and smooth of any excess with a wet finger after about half an hour. All that remains to do then is to treat the cladding to a drink of good quality preserver/stain. Apply the stain liberally, especially in the joints as they open and close in varying atmospheric conditions and may expose strips of original raw colour. The best stains are spirit based as they soak very deeply into the wood and don't form a skin on the surface so the wood can always 'breathe'. Water-based ones tend to be thicker in consistency and many form a semi-shiny skin.

OK Brits, you can put up that guttering now!

Now you can stand back and take a really good look at your brand new workshop. It's not finished yet but at least it's standing up by itself.

81

This (not very good) picture shows the work-shop after the extension was built. I simply removed the end wall and carried on building. The banana effect is camera parallax — not my building technique!

CHAPTER 8

Variants

When I first started this book the concept was very simple and based upon a totally demountable workshop. Nice idea, but the more I thought about it the more it became clear that a demountable type of building would not be the most popular in terms of general usage. So, after a considerable amount of rewriting, the original concept has been relegated to a variant of a more permanent structure. Speaking of variants – I would expect that many of the workshops built to the basic design in this book will vary from it in some way or another. That's no problem but some variations introduce complications which need a little explaining to ensure that the integrity of the finished workshop is not compromised.

Lean-to's
Building the workshop against an existing structure has definite advantages because it provides a substantial basis to build off and the finished structure will be more rigid. It is probably not worth building a wall to use for support – not unless you need a screen or a garden wall anyway – but if you do decide to then it must be built properly: the foundations should be strips of concrete 300mm wide and 150mm deep and placed on very well compacted

hardcore, generally as shown in Detail 8.1. The wall itself can be of single skin construction and should either have a return wall or have piers spaced every 2.5m to stabilise it. The piers will jut out of the wall so build them on the other side to the one that you are going to build the workshop against and don't install a DPC. (Single skin brick walls built with DPCs have a nasty habit of blowing over every time we get high winds because they are fundamentally unstable.)

The top course of bricks must be protected from frost, either by capping stones or 'soldiers' which are half bricks set vertically with the broken face set onto the wall. (Soldiers are very difficult to start because once you've balanced the first half brick in mortar on the top of the wall and then buttered up the second one, the first one has fallen over! Do it by 'sticking' two half bricks together and then set them in a bed of mortar on the wall.) Once the wall is finished allow at least a month before building against it and, if it is single thickness, attach the battens by screws and not masonry nails. For best results (as all the good recipes say) don't put the door or any windows in it.

Once you have something to build against you can't then simply build a

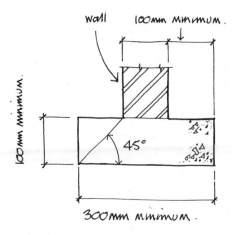

wall   100mm minimum.

100mm minimum

45°

300mm minimum.

Detail 8.1 *Typical single skin wall foundation for walls up to 2.5M in height.*

three-sided workshop and screw it thereto – not unless you like mushrooms! Walls soak up water, not just from the ground but also from rain and fog. The important thing to remember is that brick and mortar are very porous and water will not only pass easily across the thickness of a wall but, if it extends up above the roofline of the workshop, any that has soaked in higher up will drain down within the wall thickness as shown in Detail 8.2a. For the benefit of any sceptics who may believe that the risk of dampness penetrating a solid brick wall in any quantity is really very small I would point out that damp behaves in the same way as heat. If one side of the wall is dry and the other is damp, the water will move across the thickness to equalise the difference because Nature likes things in equilibrium. If you cover one side of a wall and then thoroughly dry it out by heating it, the flow of water will increase dramatically. In other words, building the workshop will increase the dampness in the non-

weathered side of the wall.

Just to make things even more complicated there are three types of brick wall: single skin garden walls (4½ in. thick), 9 in. solid as used on older house walls, and the cavity type wall as used on houses since around 1945. Normally these different types would have different solutions. There is an easy way of dealing with all of them but I should point out that in the case of the cavity wall it would be considered as a 'fix' by most architects. This is because many cavity walls are not ventilated and, as the simple solution involves placing a vapour barrier along the wall face, any water in the wall behind the barrier could become trapped. (In fact it would travel horizontally beyond the barrier and then dry out.) The only thing that I will say about using this method is that it would not be wise to use it where a high proportion or even all of a cavity wall would be obscured. The technically correct solution is to install a special horizontal barrier called a cavity tray along the full length of the lean-to as shown in Detail 8.2b. This barrier intercepts any water and discharges it through open perpends (the vertical joint between two bricks) just above the lean-to. Fitting the barrier is a major job as it is necessary to remove two courses of bricks at high level along the whole length of the lean-to. *Don't try it yourself unless you know exactly what you are doing – the removal of more than half a dozen bricks in one course without special support being provided will probably cause total failure in the wall above.* Let's do it the easy way!

Detail 8.3 shows how. It is a vertical section through the brick wall and includes not only the treatment of the wall face but also the workshop base and roof junctions to show how they should be arranged. The essential part is the vapour barrier which totally isolates the inner skin of the workshop from the brick wall face. Take special note of how it interleaves with the base DPM and how it is terminated on the roof. This will not only stop dampness working its way into the workshop but it will also stop water which has penetrated through the wall thickness and direct it down into the foundation. (I should point out that with the possible exception of very severe weather conditions with rain driving against the face of a wall, very little water would actually be involved.) The barrier must also extend beyond the workshop so that the ends can be folded round the corners and overlapped with the others in the new workshop side walls. As this barrier is against a brick wall I would suggest that you use 1000 gauge polythene instead of the normal 500 gauge.

The roof felt can't be run right over the roof for obvious reasons so stretch it up against the wall face and trim as shown in the drawing. The battens will hold it down and the flashing will prevent any weather penetration. The workshop is protected by the way the vapour barrier is lapped over the roof but it is good practice to limit the amount of water that penetrates behind the barrier.

While we're on the roof, just as there is a cheat to extend the span of joists by building in spine walls, so there is one for the mono-pitch roof. It involves installing struts at an angle of 45 degrees from the rafters across to the wall. The struts should be fitted one third of the way between the wall and the eaves (from the wall end of the roof) to a point down the wall of

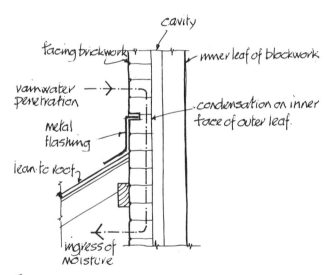

The junction of the roof with the cavity wall indicates moisture penetration caused by ineffective flashing.

Detail 8.2a *Moisture path into obscured wall.*

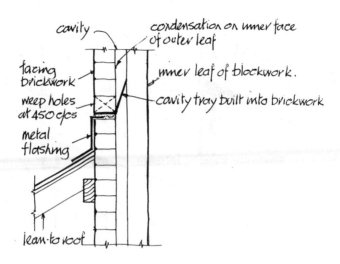

cavity

condensation on inner face
of outer leaf

facing
brickwork

inner leaf of blockwork.

weep holes
at 450 c/cs

cavity tray built into brickwork

metal
flashing

lean-to roof

The junction of the roof with the cavity wall indicates
the introduction of a cavity tray which prevents
moisture penetration into lean-to workshop.

Detail 8.2b *Cavity tray detail.*

exactly equal distance. The result is a series of struts forming a triangle between the wall and a point equal to one third of the span and it can be used to increase the span of a given rafter size by 50%. It can only be done on lean-to's though — if you do it on a free-standing building it puts an unacceptable thrust force into the wall.

The inside of the wall is then finished by an inner skin attached to the battens and the gap between can be filled with insulation as required. If the gap between the wall and inner lining is filled with insulation then technically a further barrier should be installed immediately behind the inner lining but, as I said on the same subject regarding the stud walling, it isn't

really worth the bother because the thin lining will breathe into the workshop. The only time when it must be fitted is when the lining will be prevented from breathing such as when a faced board is used instead of plain chipboard.

The base-to-wall junction shows a strip of compressible strip inserted between the two parts. The reason is that both the wall and the new base will expand and contract at different rates so to prevent localised cracking this element must be introduced. If you are installing polystyrene insulation then a strip of it will do nicely for this job.

There are many ways of joining new walls at 90 degrees to existing ones such

86

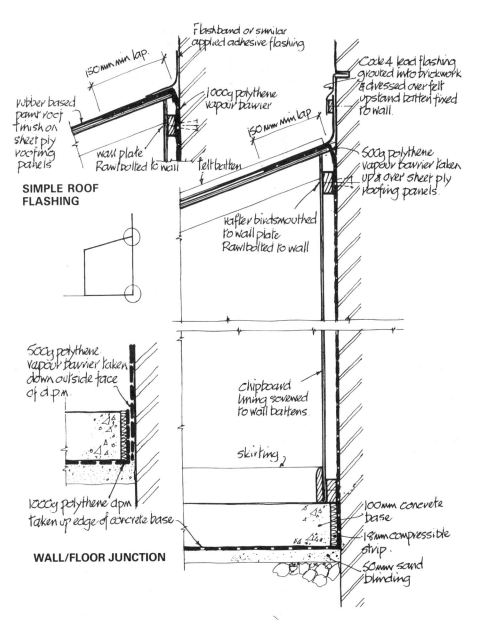

Flashband or similar applied adhesive flashing

150 mm min lap.

rubber based paint roof finish on sheet ply roofing panels

wall plate Rawlbolted to wall

felt batten

1000g polythene vapour barrier

SIMPLE ROOF FLASHING

Code 4 lead flashing grouted into brickwork & dressed over felt upstand batten fixed to wall.

150 mm min lap

500g polythene vapour barrier taken up & over sheet ply roofing panels.

Rafter birdsmouthed to wall plate. Rawlbolted to wall

500g polythene vapour barrier taken down outside face of d.p.m.

Chipboard lining screwed to wall battens.

skirting

1000g polythene dpm taken up edge of concrete base

WALL/FLOOR JUNCTION

100mm concrete base

18mm compressible strip.

50mm sand blinding

Detail 8.3 *Lean-to section showing roof and base junctions with wall.*

87

as special saddles and patented seal arrangements but these are mainly aimed at major structural joints where differential movement may occur between the old and new walls. In our context these are unnecessary and we can use the simplest method of all — vertical battens fixed to the wall face. They are the end vertical members of the new walls which are built straight off them as shown in Detail 8.4. The main verticals should be attached by screws to the brick wall but the intermediate battens for the inner lining can be fixed with masonry nails driven into the mortar joints (and not the bricks). *If you use masonry nails you must wear goggles — a mis-hit will result in them springing back out of the wall at tremendous velocity.*

As with the wall end verticals, the roof support rail (which is also called a wallplate and supports the ends of the rafters) should also be secured with screws and, as they pass through the barrier, plastic plugs and brass screws should be used. The same applies to any noggins that are fitted between the vertical battens which you are going to use as fixings for a bench or whatever. Do remember though that anything attached directly to the brick wall will transmit sound straight into the structure of which the wall is a part.

There are two other roof types which also need special construction when they form part of a lean-to arrangement — the ventilated mono-pitch and the pitched roofs. The ventilated roof is shown in Detail 8.5 and it has to be constructed in this way because there is no through route for the ventilation air so it has to escape under the verge. This is achieved by fixing spacer battens on top of the rafters and screwing the roof sheeting to them. It is still necessary to have a slot under the eave otherwise the leading edge of the roof will be starved of ventilating air.

The pitched roof poses a problem when attached to a wall in that the water will shed down the slope and saturate the wall. Detail 8.6 shows the best way of solving the problem — by means of a valley gutter. Build the pitched roof in the

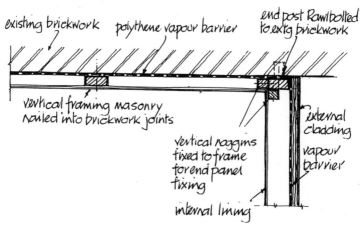

Detail 8.4 *Section through clad wall/new wall junction.*

88

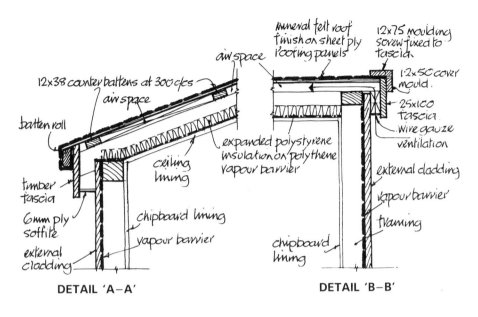

DETAIL 'A–A'   **DETAIL 'B–B'**

Labels in Detail 'A–A':
12x38 counter battens at 300 c/cs
air space
batten roll
air space
timber fascia
6mm ply soffite
external cladding
ceiling lining
chipboard lining
vapour barrier
mineral felt roof finish on sheet ply roofing panels
expanded polystyrene insulation on polythene vapour barrier

Labels in Detail 'B–B':
12x75 moulding screw fixed to fascia.
1·2x50 cover mould.
25x100 fascia
wire gauze ventilation
external cladding
vapour barrier
framing
chipboard lining

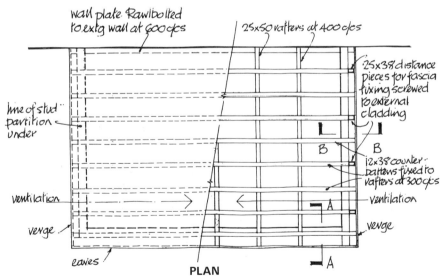

Labels in Plan:
wall plate Rawlbolted to extg wall at 600 c/cs
25x50 rafters at 400 c/cs
25x38 distance pieces for fascia fixing screwed to external cladding
line of stud partition under
B
B
12x38 counter battens fixed to rafters at 300 c/cs
ventilation
ventilation
verge
verge
eaves
A
A

PLAN

Detail 8.5 *Lean-to ventilated roof.*

89

same way as an ordinary lean-to but intercept the slope with a run of flashing which has a slight 'run' on it.

Just in case you're wondering why anyone would want to join a pitched roof to an existing wall there are three good reasons:

(1) The brick wall isn't high enough to take the high side of a mono-pitch roof.
(2) Pitched roofs always look better than mono-pitched ones and it may be desirable cosmetically.
(3) A pitched roof workshop slightly overlaps an existing wall for part of its length.

Demountable version

The modified base for the demountable version has already been covered in Chapter 6. The upper structure design has to be similarly modified in order to allow the workshop to be taken apart and then rebuilt without any major effort. It's not just a matter of arranging for the walls to be bolted together; special consideration must be given to maintaining the vapour seal within the walls as well.

Detail 8.7 shows how the vapour barrier should be wrapped around the framing and secured to it so that when bolted to the adjacent wall the two membranes join up and press together. It also shows how to arrange the corner using coach screws

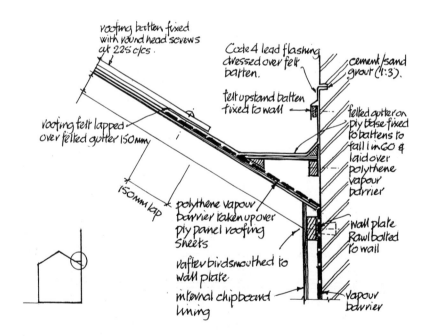

Detail 8.6 *Lean-to pitched roof details.*

90

to make the joint and then hide the heads under the corner capping strip. Coach-screws are square-headed black steel screws with a very coarse thread. You can't use coachbolts because the nut will end up behind the wall inner lining.

The roof can be arranged to be removable in several ways but the easiest is to build the walls complete with the roof slope and then fix the 'roof assembly' by means of metal brackets as shown in Detail 8.8. By roof assembly I mean the complete panels with the rafters attached and, if you're really careful, the felting as well. The brackets will show inside the finished building but they can be painted

over. (Don't be in too much of a hurry to hide the fixings because in a couple of years when you come to dismantle the thing you will never remember where they all are!)

Detail 8.8 also shows how to link a roof, be it mono-pitch or pitched, to an adjoining wall and yet be removable later. The vertical board which the rafters are attached to is hooked into an extension of the inner sheeting while the roof assembly is lowered in position. The 'gap' between the wallplate and the wall is then weathered by a flashing as shown. The flashing should extend beyond the roof by about 75mm at each end.

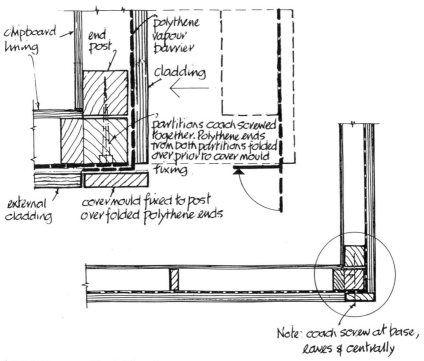

Detail 8.7 *Demountable wall junctions.*

91

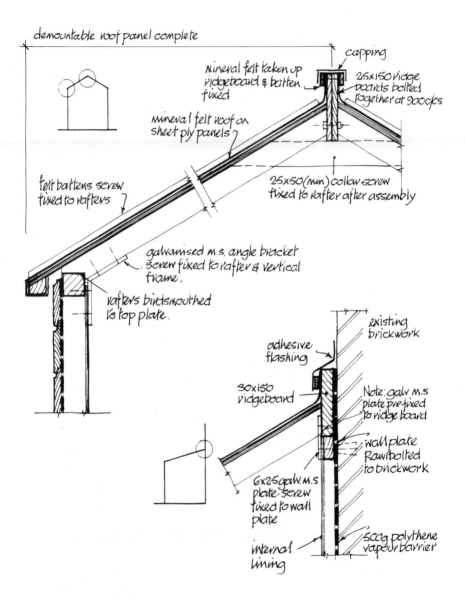

demountable roof panel complete

capping

mineral felt taken up ridgeboard & batten fixed

25x150 ridge boards bolted together at 900c/cs

mineral felt roof on sheet ply panels

felt battens screw fixed to rafters

25x50(min) collar screw fixed to rafter after assembly

galvanised m.s. angle bracket screw fixed to rafter & vertical frame.

rafters birdsmouthed to top plate.

existing brickwork

adhesive flashing

30x150 ridgeboard

Note: galv m.s plate pre-fixed to ridge board

wall plate Rawlbolted to brickwork

6x25 galv. m.s plate screw fixed to wall plate

500g polythene vapour barrier

internal lining

Detail 8.8 *Demountable roof.*

92

Proprietary demountable buildings

Having read the book this far you may be thinking that there is an easier way! If you are older than forty and lived in Britain in the 1960s you will remember the rash of pre-cast and framed garages that suddenly sprang up like weeds in everybody's garden as the spread of car ownership reached the masses. I must admit that I haven't seen one for years now but the companies that made them still trade in the business – except that are now called 'portable buildings'.

It was my intention to include some typical examples taken from a manufacturer's catalogue but to be honest the examples that I have are really naff! It may be that the catalogues in my possession are just the wrong ones and that there are more suitable structures available. What is surprising is the sheer number of manufacturers around so look in your area trade directory and phone a few up.

So what didn't I like about them? The cheapest – although not cheap as such – are just flimsy metal frames with wall panels clipped in with nasty folded metal clips; OK for a garage but not for a workshop. They do not have any provision for proper weather sealing, especially at the roof-to-wall joint, and there doesn't appear to be any easy way of lining the interior. At the top of the range and considerably better is the 'slot-together concrete panel' type. I'm sure that these units are very adequate for our purpose but you'll need a mortgage to buy one!

You could try your local shed supply company. Every area has an enterprising little company knocking out sheds for sale locally. Their products are built to a price so the construction is rather dubious with the absolute minimum of wood all joined together with staples. They can build better ones though – give them a ring and ask. You will still have to install the in-ternal lining but at least the main work will have been done.

There is one last variation in the portable building list – the Portakabin. These units are very expensive to buy initially but can be bought very cheaply second-hand either direct from large construction companies or in auctions specialising in the sale of surplus construction equipment. Not everyone will be able to use this option because in many cases either the council or the neighbours may not be too happy about the appearance of one of these things in your garden.

No matter which type of structure you choose, you will still have to provide a base for it. You can use either the wooden floor detail (6.1) or the standard concrete base detail (6.7) depending on choice. If you use a proprietary portable building be wary about using the base detail that is shown in the catalogue – the ones that I have seen are not only on the thin side but they do not include a DPC or a satisfactory seal between the walls and the base.

Garage conversions

Many people utilise the end of their garages as a workshop area and it is quite a good idea – but there are two problems. The first is security: it is extremely difficult to make a garage secure mainly because the normal exit is via the car access door and that is usually locked by a lock which came out of a Christmas cracker! If you have, or intend to have, a garage conversion, you will have to look very closely at how you can make it secure. The problem, apart from the lightweight lock, is the relative flexibility of the door and the weakness of the locking pin mountings. If possible arrange for a couple of bolts to be fitted inside the door so they can be pushed home once the car is out and you can then leave by the (securable) side access door.

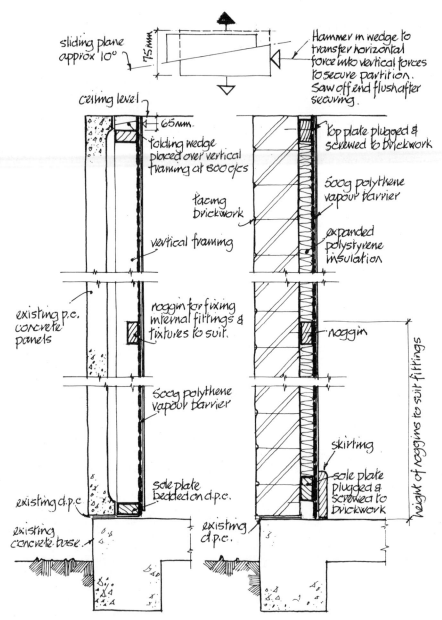

sliding plane approx 10°

75mm

Hammer in wedge to transfer horizontal force into vertical forces to secure partition. Saw off end flush after securing.

ceiling level

65mm

folding wedge placed over vertical framing at 800 c/cs

facing brickwork

vertical framing

existing p.c. concrete panels

noggin for fixing internal fittings & fixtures to suit.

500g polythene vapour barrier

sole plate bedded on d.p.c.

existing d.p.c.

existing concrete base.

Top plate plugged & screwed to brickwork

500g polythene vapour barrier

expanded polystyrene insulation

noggin

skirting

sole plate plugged & screwed to brickwork

existing d.p.c.

height of noggins to suit fittings

Detail 8.9 *Garage conversion wall details.*

94

The second problem is the perennial one of moisture. Most garages will rust tools in no time at all because of moisture migration through the structure due to the lack of a vapour barrier and, usually, a DPM. If you want paper to stay crisp and tools free of rust these two items must be installed. There are two ways of doing it – the easy and the slightly harder way. The easy way to deal with both is to build a partition wall across the garage to enclose the area and use a proprietary paint-on seal on the floor and external walls to stop moisture penetration. These liquid sealants are based on a silicone compound but are made thin enough to readily soak into the brickwork and floor. All you have to worry about then is the ceiling. In this situation I would fix battens around the perimeter of the walls at ceiling height and install a false ceiling using aluminium foil-backed plasterboard, thereby maintaining a vapour seal across the ceiling. Be careful not to encase the existing roof underside or you could be in for a lot of trouble later.

That's the easy way out but it doesn't address other problems such as the fact that garage floors are invariably rough and uneven and the very thin walls will allow an enormous amount of heat to escape. A far more satisfactory solution would be to install a false floor and to line the walls with a proper internal lining. Detail 8.9 shows a section through the wall and floor junction in such a conversion. Two ways of dealing with the lining out are shown; the first is the same as that for lining a brick wall on a lean-to and comprises a vapour barrier, battens, insulation and inner lining. The second is for situations where you either can't, or don't want to, drill into the existing walls and is especially useful for fixing a wall across the width of a garage. In this case the partitions and linings are locked in place by 'folding wedges', also shown in Detail 8.9. They are two identical taper wedges on top of each other which, when hammered from each side, produce a massive vertical jacking force. They should be positioned directly above (or under) the framing verticals and hammered home before lining out. On a floor without a DPM don't forget to fit one under the wall.

The ceiling can be as described earlier. The floor is the same as that for a base over an existing slab but with the screed only 50mm thick. Instead of a screeded floor you could lay a sheet wood floor on top of a 12mm layer of polystyrene insulation sheet. The only drawback with this method, apart from the extra work, is that there will be a slight step in the floor if the entrance door is in the new partition wall. If the door is the original garage side entrance, but it now enters into the workshop area, the step will not show as it will be below the doorsill. Assuming the former applies and you would end up with a small step in the doorway I would suggest that you fit a false sill about 75mm high in it so that you have to step over it. The reason for this is that it is small variations in floor levels that cause people to trip over – every single time that they walk over it – but large changes are stepped over without any problem at all. It's something to do with the way the brain works . . . or doesn't as the case may be!

CHAPTER 9

Fitting out

When I reached this point in the construction I remember standing in the dark, empty shell and thinking that in just a few days I would be working away in my very own purpose-built workshop. Just how wrong can someone be? It seemed to take ages and ages to do the fitting out. In fact, if my memory serves me correctly, I spent longer fitting the thing out than I actually spent building it! So what is it that takes so long and can be called fitting out? It's all the tedious bits really; like decoration, lighting, electrics, furniture, heating and finally, the floor covering. Those of you that did your internal planning early on will be able to dive straight in and start, but those that have left it until now really must sit down and get the layout sorted even if your machinery and tools are portable. You need to know what is going where so that the lights and electrical points can be positioned exactly where they are required rather than just generally spaced around the walls where you think they might be useful.

The order of events listed above follows my own fitting out sequence and I will adopt the same sequence in the notes that follow.

Decoration
Just to recap then: you should have a fully free-standing structure with a bare con-

crete floor, fully lined interior walls, fitted skirtings and complete roof with insulation infill between the rafters, and a ceiling if one is to be installed. First we must deal with the floor to give it some protection from dusting. If you intend to work off of the bare concrete in the finished workshop then I would suggest that you paint on a proprietary chemical floor finish. If, however, you intend to cover the floor when the workshop is finished then use paper or cardboard to protect it temporarily.

Now I know what you are thinking . . . "He's not actually going to tell us how to paint the thing is he?". No I'm not – well, not as such – it's just that there are a couple of wrinkles that you might be pleased to be aware of. First, fill in any gaps between the internal panels and in the corners to produce a continuous surface. Remember that this is a workshop and there probably won't be much of the walls visible in the end so don't go mad with the effort. If the workshop will be used for something like painting, electronics or some other 'quiet' occupation, use domestic fillers for this but, if the use involves banging or vibration from machinery then I would suggest that you only use one of the modern silicone based flexible fillers. That way you won't spend the next couple of years picking up strips of filler which have dropped on the floor overnight! Do make sure that the filler is paintable though as some flexible ones aren't.

Now you can paint the interior – and this single act will transform the dingy little room into a clean and very spacious workshop. Before you actually start painting you must consider the climatic situation that applies to your location as it determines the type of interior finish that you should use. The problem is that in areas where there are high humidity levels combined with large temperature fluctuations the result is usually condensation – sometimes so bad in a small room that it will run down the walls. High humidity is not only caused by a damp climate; it is also generated by confining something that breathes in a small space. So, the combination of low night-time temperatures and you breathing for hours on end with the door closed could lead to a damp, musty smelling room. If you fit this description, and if you live in Northern Europe you do, it is important that you allow the structure to absorb and give off the transient moisture which will move around in the building. Just how bad the problem will be depends on the severity of the weather conditions and the amount of moisture present. The best that you can do is to only paint the wood that you can see and to use water-based emulsion type paints rather than the impermeable gloss finish type even if the tin does say that it will allow wood to breathe. There is one little problem though – water-based paints applied on steel will cause rusting by the time the paint dries out. Now, I've already told you to attach all of the internal lining with steel screws haven't I! The answer is to dab each screw head with a brush dipped in gloss paint before painting over them with emulsion. It sounds tedious but the skirtings and window frames will almost certainly be painted in gloss so it's not as if any special effort will be required. (For more detailed information on this subject together with suggestions on how to overcome mustiness and construct a de-humidifier see my article Vapour Trouble published in the *Model Engineer*, available from Nexus Special Interests' back copies department.)

Ventilation

Following on from the comments on moisture build-up within the workshop structure, *it is very important that some form of ventilation is provided* other than an open window. This ventilation must be available all the time. Try to arrange for cool air to be drawn in at floor level and the humid air to exhaust at high level. The former can be achieved simply by not fitting a draught excluder to the door bottom edge and the latter by fitting an adjustable trickle vent such as those fitted in patio door frames. This is even more important if any combustion takes place in the workshop, either through the heating or some part of your hobby. It stands to reason that the vents should be at opposite ends of the room!

Lighting

I have a manual which was published some years ago by one of the biggest light fitting manufacturers and it was intended to provide instruction on the correct positioning and intensity of fittings for adequate light to work under. It's quite a thick book and all it really applies to is spacious, white painted rooms, such as open plan offices. As for poky, cluttered little rooms, all it really says is that there are so many interacting variables that each situation must be assessed individually. In other words without years of experience it is little short of useless. The 'variables' are:

(a) **Positioning:** the positions of the lights, their relative proximity to other light sources and to reflective and non-reflective surfaces all influence the final light level within the room.

(b) **Scatter:** the light present in a room is made up of two components – direct radiation from the source and reflected light from the internal surfaces. This is where it gets complicated because two rooms painted the same, with the same level of lighting but with different numbers or layouts of cupboards, will have different light levels!

(c) **Colour:** the colour will affect the level of light reflected not only from the ceiling but also from the walls and fittings. We all know that black absorbs all light and no-one would paint the interior of a workroom in it, but the subtle difference between two 'whites' can significantly reduce the amount of reflected light within the room. Similarly, a dark or natural wood colour to the benchtop could well absorb not only enough light to make it appear dark at the bench itself but could affect the general light level in the whole room. ('Dark' is a relative term here and could perhaps be replaced by 'not as bright as the rest of the room'.)

(d) **Texture:** the surface texture of a finish can also significantly reduce the level of reflected light by causing a colour to behave like a darker one.

(e) **Orientation:** 1 would think that the standard light fitting for all workshops must be the fluorescent fitting but the light emitted is directional, unlike a light bulb which is spherical and gives a much more uniform light spread. Flourescent lights don't emit any light from the ends of the tube so all the light in this area *must* be reflected there.

The only thing that I can say on the subject following the list above is that *you are on your own on this one!* I spent ages trying to get the lighting level right in my own workshop and I based the total wattage required on that in my kitchen which has roughly the same area (but a different shape). The kitchen has a single fluorescent fitting of 60W and is nearly as bright as I thought a workshop should be so I installed two, shorter, 40W tubes. The result was a dingy room with dark corners. In the end it took 200W to attain a satisfactory light level! The reasons for the difference in lighting requirements is a direct result of all of the items on the list above interacting with each other. The final result then was a level of around 20 (fluorescent) watts per square metre.

Before someone writes to me to complain about my use of watts as a measure of light levels I had better explain my reasons for doing so. In the 'old days' it was easy – there were only tungsten lights in general use and the power consumption (watts) was a convenient and universal method of referring to the light output. Then some cleverdick came along and invented the domestic fluorescent fitting. Instead of giving the light output in something more correct, such as candelas or lux, he chose to stick to the power consumption in watts instead – and, as we all know, fluorescent fittings use far less power for the same light output as tungsten bulbs. The result is that we still refer to the output in watts but with a qualifying statement that it is fluorescent or tungsten watts. If I started talking in lux levels it would mean nothing at all to most people reading this book. (If you do understand lux as a measure of light and can measure it in your room you should aim for a level of around 500 lux at the point of use. This means that this level should exist in the immediate vicinity of any machine and at the surface of a bench or drawingboard.)

As I stated earlier you are on your own on this one because I am no expert — even though I thought that it would be easy to become one because I had the manual! All I can offer on the subject are the results of my attempt to resolve the lighting problem in my shop:

(a) It appears to be better to use a few long fittings rather than many short ones.
(b) Twin tube fittings seem to be far more effective at spreading the light around than individual units.
(c) Try to avoid fitting the lights so that they are at 90 degrees to benches or machinery unless they are actually directly above them.
(d) Try to avoid putting the light source behind you. It may sound obvious but in a relatively narrow room the tendency would be to fit the tubes down the middle of the ceiling. That would mean that the only light on a bench facing the wall would be from reflection because you would be blocking the direct source. Better to fit them along each side of the ceiling close to the walls.

Once the basic lighting is in place and at the correct level it should strike you as very bright when you walk in — but only for a moment. Finish off by positioning spotlights local to benches and machines.

Electrics

Surely, you may say, the electrics in a workshop must demand more space than as a mere subsection of a chapter? Well, it depends really. If you just need a power supply in a simple workshop then this subsection will be more than adequate but, if you are fitting out a workshop with big machinery or power hungry equipment, then what you need is a specialist book. Fortunately for me such a book has just been added to the Nexus Special Interests' Workshop Practice Series and is entitled *Workshop Electrics* by Alex Weiss (ISBN 1 85486 107 7). My little effort in this chapter can only relate to straightforward electrics and I have assumed that those carrying out the work are reasonably competent in basic electrical matters such as fitting plugs, wiring up switches etc. *Anyone considering carrying out their own wiring should take note that the quality of materials and installation are governed by standards; in the case of Britain the IEE Regulations apply.* Don't be tempted to think that because you are the only user of the workshop then you don't have to observe them — you do — because although you might be able to work around an iffy system, those that follow you won't know about its failings.

All domestic supplies are in alternating current; the voltage and frequency may vary from country to country but the AC bit is constant. It means that the flow of electricity goes both ways, and the number of times it changes direction per second is called the frequency (or Hertz). This is important for two reasons: The first is that unlike a DC circuit the electricity will be available from both directions as there is no positive or negative and it is this that makes the ring main circuit possible. The second is that whereas with DC switching off the positive supply kills all of the power beyond the switch, with AC switching off a switch doesn't mean that the electricity is off beyond it — it is just interrupted. The misunderstanding of the characteristics of AC power is not helped by the fact that we commonly refer to the wires as 'live', 'neutral' and earth. (This has now been changed to 'phase', 'neutral' and earth, thereby removing the misleading reference to a live supply.) Both phase and neutral are live. Neutral refers to the wire's position in the circuitry of the generation and distribution system and is utterly meaningless in the context of its use in domestic wiring. The titles should be 'phase', 'live' and earth, or alternatively 'switched phase', 'live' and earth. *If you don't understand the system don't touch the wiring.*

How much?

Before you can sort out the electrical supply you will need to have a good idea of the likely power demand and the best way to do that is to count up your watts. List all of the electrical equipment that you will be using including heating, lighting, and power. Then allow for any later additions that are likely to be made. As an example let's say that you have 200W of lighting, a 1kw heater, a 1kw cutting machine and a 500W soldering iron. That lot totals 2700 watts or 2.7kw. From this you need to derive the current consumption or amps. Watts are current × voltage so, using the British 240V as an example, dividing 2700 by 240 means that the current must be 11.25 amps. This is well within the capacity of a normal domestic ring main system and so could be supplied by a similar system in the workshop. You must try to make the best assessment of the maximum demand that you can, but don't cheat because the last thing you want is an electrical fire in your new pride and joy.

If your total demand is low (just for heating and a couple of lights), let's say around 6A (1.5kw), then you could obtain your power from a fused spur from the house. If it is between 6A and 20A (5kw) then a separate fused supply from the house incomer together with a ring main in the workshop will suffice. If it is above 20A then I suggest you find a good electrician — and what are you doing anyway!

Power source

Getting power out to the workshop is not as easy as it might appear. For a start it must be readily divorcable from the house mains supply (by law) and the materials and standard of workmanship must be top quality in order to withstand exposure to the elements. *Under no circumstances should the power be derived by linking directly into the house ring main as this could lead to an overload and a fire in the house wiring.*

In the low demand case of 6A you could effectively run the supply via an ordinary extension lead providing it is fused where it joins into the house circuit. Connection could either be by a fused spur or even a simple three pin plug in one of the sockets. This method is not the best as some house circuits may be near their limit already so use this option with care and only after taking into account the existing loading on the house system. *It is very important that no matter where the power comes from it must be fused at a lower level than the rating of the source cable.*

For anything above minimal demand there is really only one place where the supply should be taken from and that is the consumer unit or main incoming fuse-board. It should have its own dedicated fuse which will not be used to supply power to any other point. Most domestic consumer units have spare ways and it is easy to fit a suitable fuse (15 or 30A) and run the supply from it. That is exactly what I did. While you are messing around with the incomer it would be an ideal opportunity to install an earth leakage trip unit. There are various types available, just ask at an electrical store or your power supply company for information. Don't underestimate the value of these devices because one could save you the embarrassment of having to be prised out of a corner of the workshop, stiff as a board and smoking lightly!

As for the power cable: no matter how many short lengths of suitable cable you may have laying around don't be tempted to join them to save a few bob. There are external joint boxes on the market but they are expensive and, unless you know exactly what you are doing, the weather will eventually get in. Pay up and buy a single run of 45A twin and earth cable long enough to do the job.

Once you've got a supply there is the problem of getting it out to the workshop. There are two ways – below ground and above it. Below ground has to be preferred because once it is (correctly) installed and buried you can forget all about it. The details of the underground conduit were given in Chapter 6 and if you are using this method all that needs to be done is to tie a strong cord to the end of the cable and pull it through. Just to make sure that the cord doesn't slip off halfway along the pipe, bare the ends of the two wires and twist them together so that you can tie the cord through the loop. If you have done the job properly both ends of the cable will be under cover – one at the fuseboard and the other inside the workshop – so you will not need to worry about weather penetration via the cable. I will repeat myself here though and remind you to mark the cable run where it crosses the garden very prominently and permanently.

If the cable must be above ground there are two ways to do it; by overhead conduit and by catenary. The overhead conduit will allow a normal two wire and earth cable to be used but a catenary can only be used with armoured cable, just in case something smashes into it! Installing an overhead conduit is self explanatory but do ensure that it is well clear of anything that may pass below it and is well and truly supported. Use domestic copper or PVC tubing and bends rather than the traditional galvanised gas barrel tubing with screwed fittings.

Catenaries are different animals altogether as it is necessary to anchor a strong steel wire between two points and then suspend the live cable from it as shown in Detail 9.1. They don't look very nice and the cable should be the very expensive steel wire armoured type rather than the conventional PVC covered one. To set one up first solidly anchor an eyebolt or strong hook into both structures and then run a woven steel cable between them, putting as much tension in it as you can. The steel cable is a bit of a problem to get hold of but you could use fisherman's trace wire – which is a superbly strong woven steel cable coated in PTFE and sold with its own ferrules for crimping the ends into loops. Trace wire is available in different breaking strains and I would purchase the strongest one that the shop stocks. The very minimum should be 75kg breaking strain. Once the catenary is up you can hang the cable under it in short loops so that it will never be subjected to any strain. The supports at each loop can be ordinary cable ties as used commercially but they should be black as the white ones brittle in sunlight. Overhead cables like this introduce a problem in that you have got to feed it into the building without bringing the weather with it. The best way is to run it down past the entry hole and then do a complete turn so that it rises back up a short way before entering the building. That way the rain runs off the cable and drips to the ground. Similarly, once it emerges into the workshop, run it vertically for a short way to prevent even small amounts of water from penetrating the internal junction box.

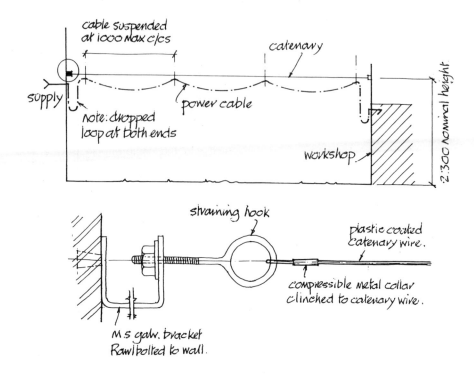

Detail 9.1 *Catenary details.*

Workshop wiring

Inside the building terminate the cable in a junction box so that it can be split off in at least three ways, one to feed the lighting and the other two for the ring main power circuit. A ring main is only a tiny bit more work to run than a spur system and its advantages are so great that you would be silly not to bother. A spur is a single cable connected to a power supply and terminating in either a socket or piece of equipment such as a tablelamp. A ring main is a cable which runs round the building via a series of outlets and then returns to the power supply point. Detail

9.2 shows the difference between the two. If you run a three core spur away from the supply and terminate it at a socket, the current that the spur can carry will be controlled by the rating of the wire. If however, you continue it round the building and connect it back onto the power supply again, the current can go both ways round, so the current that the circuit can carry will be doubled. It's pretty pointless to do this for a single outlet but where there are two or more it really does make sense. It isn't necessarily done to save money on the cable size either, the reason is because it dramatically reduces

102

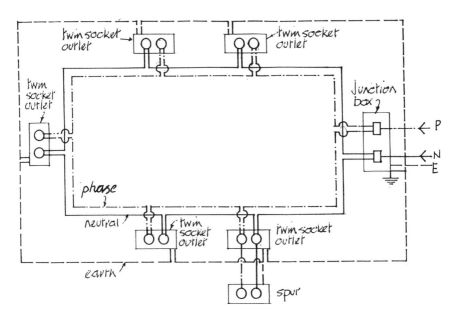

Detail 9.2 *Ring main schematic.*

the risk of an electrical fire due to a circuit overload.

Those of you that know anything about wiring will have realised that my ring main is not a true one — while the wiring inside the workshop does form a complete ring, the single supply cable makes it a spur with a ring on the end. (That's all your house is though when looked at in terms of the single supply that enters the consumer unit.) To make the system safe the supply cable must have a rating in amps greater than the demand on the whole system will be. I've already suggested that the rating should be 45A for that cable but the ones that form the ring main itself can have a lower rating — half of it in fact. In practice, unless you have a very large workshop, it would be best to run the ring in the same cable.

In our houses we go to enormous lengths to hide wiring on the grounds of aesthetics but, not only is it the devil itself to alter or extend, but if a problem does occur you won't know about it until smoke appears! I think that a workshop should only have surface run wiring (especially a wooden one) so that not only can the almost inevitable changes to the system be effected with the minimum of aggro but, if anything does get hot, you will see it before it gets out of hand. As far as looks goes, just a little care with the wiring layout with neatly spaced cable staples and nice straight runs should result in a very tidy installation. However, if you insist on nice smooth walls then by all means spend hours trying to fiddle stiff cables through tiny holes in your walls — just don't curse me! It would be much better to splash out on a surface trunking system though.

103

How you lay the system out will depend on what the building will be used for. In my workshop I am forever plugging and unplugging various tools so I set my cabling about 300mm above bench level with the outlets strategically placed near benchtops and fixed machinery. The exception to this is near the doorway where, obviously, the cable has to go 'up or under'. Mine goes under (along the back of the door sill) and, while it is down low, a couple of sockets supply the heater and a dehumidifier.

Run the cable right round the room and connect into and out of each socket as you go. Eventually you will return to the start and the end can be connected to the start − if you see what I mean. Sockets wired into the ring like this can be double outlets but those on the end of a spur should only be single outlet ones. It is not wise to increase the number of outlets by means of multiway adapters unless they are fitted with a single fuse for all of the outlets.

The lighting side is easy; just run a supply cable from the workshop incomer junction box via an in-line 5A fusebox and then on to the lights through a normal single pole domestic lightswitch. Inside the switch cut the outer sheath off and cut through the phase wire and connect it through the switch (thereby creating the 'switched phase'). Continue the cable up into the first light terminal block and then via a jumper cable on to the next one, and so on until all of the lights are looped in. It is not necessary to complete the circuit to form a ring main if there are only a few lights.

If the workshop is the demountable version, don't forget to allow for later removal when installing the electrics and equipment. In the case of the electrics it may be as well to fix the cables, junction boxes and light fittings to the underside of the roof with loops fed down the walls to the sockets and light switch. Alternatively, terminate the cables at the corners of each wall in a junction box and run a short 'jumper' between them so that it's easy to disconnect them later.

Finally, electricity is possibly the most dangerous thing in any workshop. A lathe might tear your arm off and a saw might lighten your hand by a few digits but a quick fry on the end of a 240V cable will usually be terminal! Always remember this and design your system accordingly. For example, if you use your workshop as a photo darkroom or other process involving water or liquids, only install pullcord operated switches and waterproof sockets. *If you don't, one day you will reach out in a blind panic to switch something on that you should have turned on earlier and . . .*

Furniture (cupboards, shelving and benches)

All that I can offer on this subject are a few ideas on the type of furniture you can use and some suggestions about storage.

If you like working with timber and have some cash left after building the workshop, the ultimate solution must be to design and construct a layout specifically tailored to your pursuit. For most of us it will be a case of make do and mend (no I'm not that old; my mother was always saying it!). A good start is kitchen base units. These are incredibly cheap, even if bought new (but without the decorative doors which cost a fortune), and can often be had for nothing if you can locate a friend or workmate who is refitting his kitchen and needs an extra pair of hands. The only problem with these units is that they usually come as flatpacks and, unless severely restrained, will return to that state at the earliest opportunity! The drawers and shelves in these units are just not man enough to take the heavy piles of spares, useful items and essential oddments that workshops seem to attract. Especially suspect are the runners and bottom panels in drawers, and the thin blockboard shelves fitted in most units. Either beef them up now (before the bottom drops out) or throw them away and make your own.

Benchtop materials can be very expensive. The best material has to be solid hardwood around 25mm thick – but you won't have any lying around just waiting for you to find a use for it. There is a cheap source though – find a disguise, slip out early on a Saturday without saying where you are going and take a very roundabout route to a jumble sale. Your objective is old sideboards, dining tables, dressers etc. as many of these dark brown, incredibly ugly pieces of furniture have good solid tops on them. You don't want the carcass so you can smash the thing up in the car park, dump the spoil and salvage just the top – after all you don't want to be seen dragging a 1940s sideboard up your front garden do you? If that's just asking too much of you the next best alternative is kitchen worktops. There are several types but probably the most common is made from high density chipboard around 38mm thick, 600mm wide and covered in an almost indestructible layer of moulded veneer. I didn't list it as my first choice simply because you will either have to pay the going rate for it or have to make do with a second-hand piece – probably with a very naff imitation tile effect on it!

You can never have enough cupboard or shelf space so make the effort during fitting out to install as many as you possibly can. While stripping your friend's kitchen take his old wall cupboards as well. The shelves will suffer the same deficiencies as those in the base units but the carcasses will be very useful. The easiest way to beef the shelves up is to install the cupboards without any back-panels and put wall brackets under all of the shelves and the bottom to stop them from drooping. Alternatively (and also suitable for ordinary shelving), replace the thin shelves with old floorboards cut to length.

One area which is always a nuisance in any workshop is the storage of long items such as raw materials. If there is a spare corner fit two or three pieces of timber diagonally across it to form a triangle where long items can be stood. Don't completely box it in though because as soon as you do your smallest and most expensive tool will jump in there and hide! No corner? Leave a small gap between two adjacent base units and partition it vertically in two or three places. Then you can put long items at the back and shorter ones in the front. Remember not to run the partitions right down to the floor.

Heating

There aren't many convenient ways of heating a small building and, although we will look at the alternatives, you will probably be left with only one method – electricity. I don't know what it costs on the Continent but it's not cheap where I am so I don't waste it. If you do end up with electric heating it is worth investing in two types of plug, one with a timer and another with a built-in thermostat. Then you can just switch on and forget it, rather than switching on an uncontrolled supply – and forgetting it! There are several types of heater available but the operative word must be 'convenient' – and very few are. The types which could be used in a small workshop are:

Portable gas heaters: these units are very effective although they can be expensive to run and some people will find it a nuisance to have to refill the gas bottle at a gas refill station. Those are the good points! Here's the not-so-good side: They must only be used in a well ventilated area; are not suitable for small rooms; can produce vast quantities of water vapour (depending on the gas mix being burnt) and shouldn't really be left unattended and, as with all flame producing heaters, incorrect adjustment or poor maintenance could result in lethal fumes. They take up floorspace, definitely cannot be tucked away and a gas bottle is a beautiful bomb. It's bad enough for the workshop to catch fire, but if it then demolishes the whole street as well!!! Frankly, unless you have a very large workshop I would not recommend using one of these units.

Paraffin heaters: much the same as gas heaters as far as the comments go but with two additions; firstly, paraffin, properly called kerosene, always produces enormous amounts of water when it burns; and secondly, it spills. Knock one of these things over and you can definitely kiss goodbye to your latest project — and your workshop!

Central heating: if the workshop is joined to or within a metre of the house I would definitely consider extending the central heating into it. As it would be beyond the reach of the house thermostat any radiators used should be fitted with thermostatic valves. For a workshop of 10 sq.m a single double radiator of approx. 1 metre square will suffice. (Read it again very slowly and it will make sense!)

Radiant heaters: the really good thing about the modern versions of what is really just an electric bar heater is that they can be fixed at high level so they don't take up valuable floorspace and there's no risk of dropping things on them or leaning on them. They are very effective but the heat can be very harsh. They should not be used where there could be a lot of combustible airborne dust (as in a wood turning workshop) or you could discover that combustible also means explosive! Fine dust and red hot wires do not mix — well, not for long anyway!

Convection heaters: take a radiant heater, hide the hot wires behind a screen, and you have a convection heater. These units are quite effective, more so if fan assisted, but they are usually floorstanding and so take up space.

Fan heaters: I use a fan heater mounted high up on a wall to provide a quick way of warming up my own den. The heater is actually a large hairdrier and, coupled with a normal floor mounted convection heater, heats my workshop a treat. Many types are available at relatively low cost.

Oil-filled radiators: I'm not sure whether these are designed to be a primary source of heating but they would be ideal for secondary heating if coupled with a fan heater or other 'quick warm-up' device. One nice thing is that they are fitted with thermostats — mainly to stop them from exploding really — but useful for heat control! I am an ardent scanner of the small ads in the local paper and have noticed that they can be purchased very cheaply second-hand. They are available with fan assistance but I think that the effect is still best suited to background heating.

The floor

You will probably have decided long ago what floor covering will be fitted, either because your hobby dictates a certain type, or simply because you know what would be best in your situation. It is not a good idea to work off bare concrete so, even if you are quite happy with the idea of a bare floor, you should still provide some sort of seal to inhibit dusting and limit dirt staining. In the paragraphs on decoration I mentioned the use of floor paints so I won't repeat it here.

The most obvious floor coverings are vinyl sheeting and tufted or loop carpet. Both can be purchased as offcuts very cheaply and both can be laid on sheet polystyrene for comfort and insulation. One word on the fitting of this type of floor covering though. From bitter experience I know that all sorts of things tend to get knocked over in workshops. After a very short time a combination of enamel paint, liquid bitumen and red hot items dropped during soldering made my floor look like one from a British Rail workshop! Eventually it had to be replaced and boy, how I wished I hadn't stuck the wretched thing down. It was an absolute devil to get up again — mind you, it didn't help that the biggest machine also stood on it! If your floor is also likely to suffer try to follow the two rules of not fixing the covering down in anything but a temporary way and to cut the covering to go round immovable items. Once I had learnt the lesson I cut a long strip of floor covering (not forgetting that my workshop has all of the benches and machines along one side) and just applied a little adhesive at the very ends.

There is one other covering that can be used — sheet plywood as previously described for the false wood floor. It would be best laid on a thin sheet of insulating polystyrene to give a nice 'feel' and, if damage is likely, with adhesive only used where two sheets butt together, and only then if you are likely to walk on the join. The ply sheets can be held in place by the skirtings all around the edges. 12mm ply will do at the minimum and it would be best to seal it to stop stains and splintering. The best seal is a decent varnish thinned 50:50 with white spirit and brushed on liberally. Apply two coats and the floor will be sealed but shouldn't shine.

It's done! You now have a complete workshop all ready and waiting to be used. Look after it by occasionally checking on the condition of the weatherboard that protects the bottom of the wooden structure and reseal the exterior wood every five years or so. If for any reason a leak does appear fix it as soon as you can. Apart from those minor points. . .
Enjoy it!

CHAPTER 10

Security

People involved in creative hobbies have a gift which is often the envy of many people around them – the ability to create something beautiful from raw materials or sundry components. These creations are more than just functional pieces of kit; they often embody the builder's spirit (and very often quite a few years of his life!). To *not* lose such a creation to the likes of a petty criminal must be priority number one for all creative artists. The moral? Look very closely at your workshop security then reach into your pocket and protect it as you would your own family. This won't completely guarantee immunity but if the worst does happen you will at least be able to put your hand on your heart and say that you did all that was possible to prevent it. There are already far too many people out there saying "If only I'd . . . "

Have you ever watched one of those wildlife programmes where a herd of gazelles stand around and wait for the lions to pick one of them for lunch? They are following the principle that the sheer number of them reduces the odds of an individual animal becoming the victim. It makes about as much sense as the whole population of a town crowding round a lunatic with a gun to reduce the odds of

being shot! Now we're not that daft are we? We would either remove the problem or be somewhere else wouldn't we? Sadly that is not the case; it seems that many of us could do with feeling the tops our heads to see if there are two pointy things sticking out because we leave ourselves wide open to attack all the time – and with the number of 'lions' steadily increasing the odds of being the victim are getting progressively shorter and shorter.

The 'lions' in this context are burglars. They are very well aware of our general laxity on the subject of security – indeed, they rely on it. This laxity doesn't just relate to the level of security that we fit to our property though, it also applies to our basic attitude towards the problem. We all know that burglars aren't masked characters in striped jerseys and carrying bags with swag written on them, but for some reason we seem to believe that they only operate under cover of darkness – and only use our security then. It may surprise you to learn that the majority of break-ins occur during the daytime, often while someone is still in the property (down the garden), or while the owner has just popped down the shops.

Garage, shed and outbuilding break-ins are very common indeed. They are generally easy to enter and the items that they contain are easily disposed of. Unfortunately this means that workshops are likely targets – not because they are workshops but because they are mistaken for ordinary outbuildings containing highly saleable domestic bits and pieces such as lawnmowers, kids bikes etc. Once inside, and even on finding that the contents are specialised and of little 'street value', the thief is very unlikely to leave empty-handed.

As far as our workshop is concerned we need to worry about three types of criminal:

(a) **The opportunistic thief**
(b) **The ordinary burglar**
(c) **The 'specialist' thief**

All three are bad news and they have to be dealt with in different ways. In theory, if you take the necessary precautions against all three, you should be reasonably safe. Most people don't protect themselves as I've already said and, rather perversely, we can use this 'aiding and abetting' of Mr. Average to our advantage as a defence against at least two of the criminal types. Before going into the sort of precautions that you should take for each threat there is one thing that you can do that will help in the fight against all three: join your local Neighbourhood Watch. Many people are cynical about these schemes but the truth is that they have one massive advantage over all other types of policing – local knowledge. If you are over 30 years old you will probably remember the days of the local bobby on his 'Noddy bike'. These bobbies operated over a much smaller area than the individual policeman does today and, as a result, he got to know all of the faces that fitted into his patch. Those days have gone and so has the local knowledge that the bobby had. Neighbourhood Watch

members either already have, or they quickly gain, a knowledge of the people who belong in their area. *Faces which don't belong are taken notice of.*

So let's take a close look at each of the threats and see what you can do to minimise the chances of being a victim.

The opportunistic thief

This type of criminal relies on one simple fact – that people do not believe that they could be burgled in the time it takes to make a cup of tea so they don't lock up. Let me assure you – you can. In the rest of this chapter I shall attempt to give advice on the type of security measures that can be fitted to a workshop, but there is very little that I can do about vigilance. It is only vigilance that offers the best protection against what is probably the most prolific of criminals, the opportunistic or walk-in thief. *Always remember that the greatest number of burglaries occur during the hours of daylight and each one takes but a few minutes. So, if you're not in it – lock it! Even the very best locks are absolutely useless if you haven't turned the key.*

In order to be vigilant you have make a simple psychological change – accept that you will probably be burgled one day. Always bear it in mind and never leave tools openly visible, or the workshop open and unlocked while you are indoors, or even while you are in the veg patch. Just consider how long it would take to walk into your workshop, pick up just one item, such as an electric drill, and walk out: seconds. I can personally vouch for the way that these crooks operate because one plagued my own area for some time. Anything left in the garden while we weren't around would simply disappear. My own builder's level went that way – together with the bulbs out of the garden lights! The police eventually caught him and I got my level back but I was very lucky.

There are some positive things that you can do to reduce the chances of receiving a visit. Some were included in the chapter on planning but I will repeat them again:

(a) If at all possible position the work-shop away from open view. If this just isn't possible then destroy any sight line into the windows or door by positioning a screen or wall.

(b) It is an enormous advantage if the workshop is close to the house as this restricts the thief both in terms of the noise he can make and the amount of head start he will have if detected. The last thing that he needs is a very rapid response by you.

(c) Don't think that these characters need an open door as an invitation to burgle. They will walk in and try a door to see if it is unlocked. If it is then you're about to lose something.

(d) While a thief may only take one item, that item may be the very thing that you have spent three or four years building or, perhaps even worse, it may be something that you don't use very often and its disappearance may not be noticed immediately. In fact, you may never realise that you have been burgled!

The ordinary burglar

There are many burglars around that specialise in breaking into outbuildings. The low risk, grossly inadequate security and highly saleable proceeds are clearly attractive to the criminal types. The only defence is to install effective security devices to the door and window openings — *and to use them*. It is said that a skilled burglar can get into most houses in Britain (and probably elsewhere in the world), in less than two minutes simply because the average level of protection is woefully insufficient. Note that I'm talking about house burglary — so what level of security would normally be on an outbuilding?

It is worth pointing out that while no-one is immune to being burgled, some are at far greater risk than others. The security measures that follow will result in a reasonable level of protection. I have no doubt that this level will be insufficient for some areas where even steel shutters and a thick mesh grid in the roof may not deter the thief. (Some ideas on protection against extreme threats are given later in this chapter.) Be very careful about making your own assessment of what is required as potential victims invariably underestimate the true risk. For advice call the Crime Prevention Officer at your local police station and he will advise you based on crime levels in the area.

So what is a reasonable level? In theory it is one that is sufficient to make the criminal look elsewhere. The trouble is that this isn't as simple as it sounds because burglars don't look at things in quite the same way as you and I. What most of us would consider to be well protected probably isn't because while you will reinforce all the obvious places the burglar will know of other ways of getting in that you will not have thought of. There is an example of this in the section on doors later in this chapter. There is also a difference in approaches in that you may fit a security device but will fail to test its effectiveness simply because you may cause damage to say, the window frame. Thieves are no respecters of property and will have no qualms about ripping the whole frame out if that will get them where they want to be.

Before looking in detail at the various ways of protecting the workshop itself there are a few fundamentals which can reduce the risk of being burgled in the first place:

(a) One of the best ways is to make it very obvious that there is protection and so difficult to get round that the thief will look for easier pickings. If an adequate level of security has been installed on a house the burglar will only find out on attempting to break in as they tend to be hidden for cosmetic reasons. So, while our house security may be discreet, on the workshop decent ironmongery and even bars at the windows are not such a problem.

(b) We all do odd jobs for friends or people we know in the pub but it isn't necessary to go into detail about the machines that you have or the models you have built — you never know who is listening. Similarly, don't leave your pride and joy sitting on the front lawn or sticking out of the back of the car while having a break. The fewer people that know about you the less the chance of becoming a victim.

(c) If possible you can try to hide the very existence of the workshop by very careful siting in the garden but do not be fooled into thinking that disguise is a good way of avoiding being burgled. As stated earlier; secrete your workshop as a simple shed or in an unprotected garage at your peril.

(d) One insurance agent I spoke to said that it is estimated that anything up to half of the houses in this country have a key secreted within 10m of the door it fits — and guess who knows it?

(e) Always lock up properly, even if you expect to be out for just a few minutes.

(f) Always check that you have locked up.

Let's look at a typical workshop and analyse each risk area in detail. At this point I would like to thank the Chubb Security Company for allowing me to reproduce some examples of their security equipment to illustrate the text. I should point out that I have no connection with the company.

The door

The most obvious point of entry is the door because it is a most difficult opening to make fully secure. Where the workshop is directly connected to the house a second door could be cut into the house wall and then the 'normal' door locked and bolted from inside the workshop. For most situations though this probably won't be the case so we will have to do our best to secure it from the outside. First on the list *must* be a decent lock and it must be a deadlock. This means that the bolt cannot be forced back into the casing when it is locked and the whole thing is of armoured construction. Then there is the question of the number of levers. They commonly come in 5 or 7 lever types and the difference is that the 5 lever type has fewer key combinations — around 1000 as against the 7 lever's 6000 or so. To my mind 5 levers are adequate for most situations. Maximum security will be achieved with a lock fitted within the door thickness or on the inside of the door itself. For doors which do not have lock recesses there are high security padlocks and pad bars available which result in a similar level of security to the deadlock. Detail 10.1 shows a suitable deadlock and Details 10.2 and 10.3 show the equivalent in padlock and pad bar technology.

With such a lock fitted most people would think that the door is secure, but it isn't. The burglar won't bother with the lock at all. He will just jemmy open the hinge side! Next on the list then is to protect the hinge side and an obvious thing to do is to fit substantial hinges.

111

Latch is a simple latch.
Lock is a latch and deadlock.
Deadlock is a single deadlock.

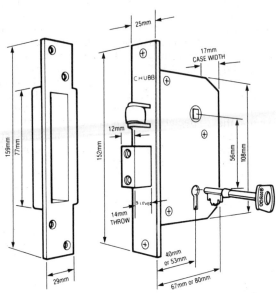

Detail 10.1 *5 lever mortice lock.*

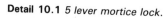

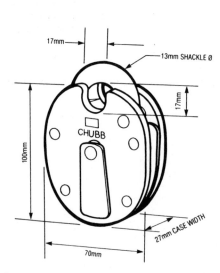

Detail 10.2 *Cruiser padlock.*

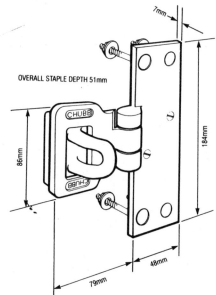

Detail 10.3 *Heavy duty padbar.*

112

Most conventional butt hinges are hopelessly inadequate both in construction and method of securing, especially when used on outward opening doors. If you are stuck with using this type then only use ones made from good steel plate and buy the biggest you can find. Biggest relates to the length, and therefore the screw hole spacing, rather than to the thickness of the metal. Use the longest screws that the frame will accept and I don't have to tell you to drill pilot holes to prevent the frame from being massively weakened by splitting, because you would anyway — wouldn't you? Outward opening doors are especially weak on the hinge side because the edge of the door is exposed. Such doors need a little more than decent hinges.

An alternative and far stronger hinge is available called a tee or plate hinge as shown in Detail 10.4. Hang the door on two of these with coachbolts right through both the frame and the door and the casual burglar won't even bother to get the jemmy out! (It is important that these hinges are through bolted with round headed coachbolts and not woodscrews or coachscrews even if they have special heads.) In higher risk areas it may be advisable to fit three such hinges.

If you decide to use decent conventional butt hinges complete with long screws the hinge side will still be suspect and should be backed up with additional protection in the form of steel security bolts as shown in Detail 10.5. They are fixed steel bolts set into the door or frame near each hinge and are called hingebolts. As the door is closed the projecting pins engage in special sockets and they transfer the defence from the hinges to the hardened steel bolts. They are absolutely essential for outward opening doors.

Detail 10.6 shows a retractable version for fitting on the opening edge of a door and they are called mortice doorbolts. In this type the bolt runs in a tube set in either the door or frame and a socket accepts the bolt in the closed position. They are much stronger than ordinary doorbolts because they use the thickness of the door for support rather than a few tiny screws. A slight drawback when used on doors which are only locked from outside is that as they are operated by a splined key and the keyhole will be visible. Mind you, the hole is tiny and can be kept discreet.

There is one situation where the intruder might still try to open the door on the lock side even when deadlocks are fitted. That

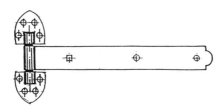

Lengths: 300mm to 1200mm in increments of 50mm.
to 750mm and then in increments of 150mm
to 1200mm.

Detail 10.4 *Heavy reversible T-hinge.*

113

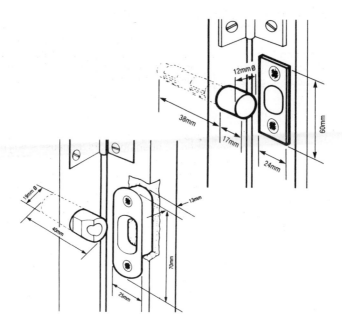

Detail 10.5 *Hinge bolts.*

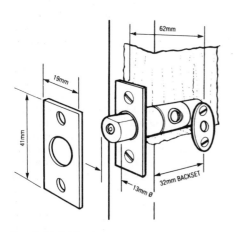

Detail 10.6 *Mortice door bolts.*

is when the frame looks like it may be of softwood or insubstantial hardwood. If you have just spent good money on new locks then for goodness sake make sure the frame is up to the job. Similarly, the lockplates or escutcheons are often fitted by tiny screws little more than 12mm long. *These little plates are very important and an insufficient fixing could well nullify the whole lock's effectiveness.* Make sure that this bit is very well fixed and, if you suspect that the door frame might not be up to scratch, extend the plate by silver soldering it to a much longer plate that you can get several screws into. Use the longest screws possible to fix it to the frame. Just a few notes on screws:

(a) Many hardwoods eat steel screws! Always use good quality brass or stainless steel ones for fixing the locks etc. and always drill a pilot hole first.

114

(b) When using brass screws, first run a steel screw in and then replace it with a brass one.

(c) Steel screws can be very difficult to screw into some hardwoods — and twice as difficult to get out later! Dip the screw into lard or fat before screwing it in.

(d) Always remember that woodscrews are for joining wood, not for high security fixings. This applies especially when used with conventional doorbolts. The problem with them is that once they have been forced a little way their grip collapses by virtue of the taper. Such fixings are best made with long parallel screws such as self tappers which have a grip proportional to their length.

If you have followed the advice given you should now have a very secure door — or have you? What about the door construction? Many are double panelled, with the upper one glazed and the lower one fitted with a thin wood panel. The window will be covered in the next section but the lower panel is often just a panelled in window section. In other words the panel is just a bit of ply no thicker than the glass would be. Put your foot right in the middle, give it a really good push and ten to one it will pop out! Replace the panel with something more substantial which is both screwed and glued into place. Alternatively, back the thin panel up with a sheet of steel screwed or bolted in place from inside.

Right, the door is now as strong as a wooden door ever will be, now for the windows.

Windows

Windows have glass and glass breaks very easily. (I know, I know, but if I hadn't said it the next sentence wouldn't have made

sense!) There are three ways of dealing with this: use security glass (which is usually opaque); make sure that the window opening is too small to get through; fix an obstruction on the inside to prevent entry. The following advice is based on the three points above but looks at specific areas.

Looking at the door first: a door window is very convenient, especially in outward opening doors, because it will prevent you from opening it when the Management is about to bring in your tea ration! So, if there is a window try to reduce its size to a maximum of 300mm square. If it must be bigger then glaze it with Georgian wired, reinforced glass or even one of the near indestructible plastics such as Macralon. Even then fit a bar on the inside to stop the whole glass sheet being pushed in.

I would also avoid using putty on the outside as the only method of holding the glass as the burglar that broke into my brother's house did so by removing it, followed by the glass, and then reached in and opened the window! My own windows are 'stuck in' with a flexible silicon and the panes were inserted from the inside. If the glass must be fitted from outside, (because the frame was made that way), fit wood beading retainer strips and then putty over them.

Most people will want their ordinary windows to open but that means that a locking mechanism must be fitted. The weakness with all such devices is the fixings as they are invariably fixed to the frame — that simply splits when brute force is applied. In the case of a workshop the best thing to do is to assume that the glass will be broken or the frame forced open and arrange for another anti-entry device to prevent access. Bars are probably the best. They are visible and therefore a good deterrent and if fitted correctly can be immensely strong. *Always fit them on the inside because if the burglar can get a good hold on them there is every chance he will get them off.* A simple angle iron frame with bars every 150/200mm will be fine. Make the bars from gas barrel tube at least 15mm diameter and fix the frame well away from the window area so the burglar can't simply look in after breaking the glass and undo the fixings. If you don't want to feel as if you're in a prison make the bars horizontal.

If you really do object to bars of any sort then fix shelves right across the window starting as far away from the window edge as you can. It is possible that a burglar might force them off but it will be incredibly noisy, especially if your shelves fill up with the same sort of miscellanea as mine do! If you need or like the light from the window then just don't put anything on them immediately in front of the glass. It stands to reason of course that you won't put anything on them to actually encourage a break-in.

Double-glazed units can have some really good locking mechanisms with the handle operating top and bottom bolts from inside the frame, much like the secret bolts mentioned earlier. The trouble is that an automatic centre-punch will make short work of the toughened glass fitted into them so you will still need bars on windows big enough to get through.

If you have secured the door and windows and the main structure of the workshop is well constructed then you can consider that you have done your utmost to discourage entry. Normally the door and windows will be the only breaks in the building fabric but if you add any others make sure that they are suitably protected. I'm thinking of the sort of flap or low level opening which a train enthusiast may use to roll his loved creation into the workshop for servicing. Unless it

is very small treat it like a door and secure it properly with a drop-in bar from inside (like a Wild West fort gate), or make it from steel, coachbolt the runners that it runs in and lock it with a steel pin.

Non-physical deterrents

We live in a high-tech world just brimming with all sorts of equipment which will purport to protect your property. They don't — you still need to have conventional anti-burglar devices fitted otherwise all the technology will tell you is that you have just been burgled! It is possible that proximity lights or the presence of an intruder alarm box on the wall might deter a burglar but I wouldn't bet on it. Burglars tend not to hang around for too long and they know that by the time you or the police have reacted they will be down the road. *They also know that only very brave men will confront an intruder, especially at night.*

For those who want the additional security there are several systems available as follows:

(a) Proximity lights: these switch on automatically if someone approaches within a certain distance but unfortunately the all too obvious detector will tell the crook that you didn't switch the light on. They are of no use if you or the rest of the street are unaware that the thing has triggered — except that it means the burglar will not have to hold his torch! Because these units switch the power on to the lamp you could tap into this and use it to ring a bell or siren inside the house and the thief may well run for it empty handed. Don't forget though that in daylight the proximity unit switches off so it can't be used for daytime protection. Similarly, if you are out, the system is useless.

(b) Self-switching lights: these units switch the lights on at random intervals during the hours of darkness. They are of dubious use in this context because they are intended to be used where the intruder cannot actually see whether the lights were turned on by a person or automatically. It would only take a glance through the window to confirm that the place is empty and they may even assist the burglar as he will get a good look at the contents while he's breaking in!

(c) Intruder alarms: these systems have developed very rapidly over the years and can be obtained at reasonable cost. There are basically two types: one is the conventional switch type where you wire every opening to the central unit; the other is the wave interference (infra-red or ultrasonic) type that detects any movement within the protected area.

They do have drawbacks. All variations have an 'on delay' that allows rightful entry to disarm the system (so you can get in) but, as the disarming can involve punching in a code, delay periods of around 45 seconds are common. This means that by the time the alarm sounds the burglar is not only inside but has probably grabbed what he wants. He can come back later for anything else he has seen but not had time to grab! There is also a credibility problem with of these types of alarm — people just ignore them! *So if you are out the chances are that no-one else will respond to your alarm ringing until several hours later when they phone the police to complain about the noise!*

A further weakness in these systems is that they are powered by electricity and if the workshop power supply cable is clearly visible then one good yank could render your security system null and void. If you fit such a system ensure that it has battery back-up and a power supply failure-on trigger. The alarm may not be as loud on the back-up system as on full power though and it will tend to go off every time there is a power cut.

It is possible that many people buy these units in the belief that the very high decibel rating of the alarm will drive out any intruder. It is true that intense noise can be very painful but a burglar will be prepared for it; he's seen it all before.

You may have got the impression that I am not over enamoured with these systems, and you would be right. I do believe that for the purpose of protecting a workshop, effective prevention of entry is far better than any sort of rear-guard action.

The 'specialist' burglar

This sort of thief is a totally different kettle of fish to the opportunistic or ordinary burglar type just discussed. When a model or a particular piece of machinery is stolen it always suggests to me that the victim was targeted, probably by someone who has a similar interest. Stealing a 100kg train is no mean feat and there has to be a specific reason for doing so. The burglar (or his paymaster), also has to have the knowledge and the facilities to either use or dispose of the thing profitably.

The awful thing about this crime is that the thief will not only know who you are, he will know where you live, where your workshop is and what it is you have that he wants to steal. It is quite possible that he may even have looked your workshop over, possibly even with you being there, but more likely at night or when you are out. I stated earlier that part of the battle against crime is secrecy but hobbyists are usually incredibly sociable people. Those that build locomotives for instance, take them to the local track, give everybody rides and talk to anyone who asks about their hobby. It only takes one thief to identify you as the bloke from the green house or whatever and your model could be on its way out of your life.

The real problem with this type of thief is his determination. He will have planned the theft, taking into account the location and access to the workshop, together with some method of carrying the spoils. He will already know about your regular Saturday visit to the supermarket with your wife; that you disappear up the pub on certain nights of the week and that every Friday at 8 pm. you go to the Society clubhouse. In this sort of situation I'm not sure that there is much you can do to protect your workshop from being broken into. Once its existence and location are known then you have a very difficult problem as this type of burglar is not going to be put off by a few dead-locks, secret bolts, flashing lights or expensive alarm systems. Two or three good blows with a sledgehammer will split the door from top to bottom and in less than two minutes both he and your model will be gone. If he attacks during the day while you are out the chances are that no-one else will take a blind bit of notice because you are always banging anyway!

In this situation I can only offer three defences:

(1) **Secrecy:** I know from what I have already said that it is very difficult to keep your hobby a secret but always be aware that there are certain times when your workshop location is liable to become known to people that you don't know. Transporting models should be carried out discreetly so don't leave the thing half hanging out of the back of the car while you have a break. Nor should you give your address to people who say that they are interested in starting in the hobby. It just isn't worth it. Send them to the local Model Society meeting instead.

(2) **The vault:** banks are strong buildings with all sorts of defensive mechanisms to prevent unwanted entry, but that doesn't mean that they leave the money lying all over the place! They stash it in the vault. So why not have one of your own? If you can build a locomotive then a steel box with high quality padlocks and a floor of 150mm thick concrete should be a doddle. Just pop the old Choo Choo in there when it's not in use and it should be pretty safe.

(3) **The decoy:** there is a lot to be said for not even putting the model where the thief will think it should be. How about a steel box set in your garden disguised as say, a cold frame?

The above relates, as you can see, to model engineers but the same applies to every hobby where the end result is something that somebody else will want to own or sell.

Extreme threats

All of the foregoing should result in a reasonable level of protection for the average workshop but what about situations that have extreme threats? I'm thinking of those people that live in highly built up areas where petty crime seems to be part of every boy's education. The workshop in these areas will be remote from the house (where the owner lives in a flat) and probably very exposed. The same applies to clubhouses where they are remote from the rest of civilisation and just waiting for the local crooks to practice on before they move into more glamorous activities — like armed robbery! Then there is the threat from the other social misfit — the vandal.

Vandalism: dealing first with 'simple' vandalism (because outright vandalism needs the protection of the extreme threat precautions that follow). This is where the vandals are not necessarily interested in gaining entry — not when they can burn it down! The two things that these people really like are paint and fire, and the one thing that they don't like is glass. The first thing they do is break all of the windows and then totally deface all of the walls in record time. When they've finished on the paint job they will probably set fire to it. Clearly a wood structure in these areas is not likely to last long so at least the outer skin must be of brick or block construction. The designs given in this book are therefore definitely not suitable for this kind of location.

To upset their plans on the painting the most easily arranged deterrent is pebble dash. This was used extensively by local councils on houses built in a hurry just before WW2 because the bricks used for the walls were unfaced and of very poor quality. The rendering gave a decorative and weatherproof finish to the walls. In our context the rendering should be done with the biggest pebbles that the render will stand — it really does mess up the aerosol spray pattern!

To protect the windows they can be covered by heavy mesh grills but to be honest you would be better off fitting full shutters as described in the full works that follows.

The full works

The full works must cover two eventualities — entry and destruction.

In the case of sustained and extreme attempts to gain entry the only thing that can be done is to totally armour the exterior to the point where if you lose the keys you will never get inside again! I have had experience of the extreme threat situation because two business associates of mine own a metal fabrication works in Stockport where this sort of crime is considered normal. They moved their works to new premises and the office was a single storey building built as an annexe onto the factory exterior. The wooden door was protected by a deadlock and mesh anti-vandal screens covered the windows. Soon after setting up in the new office it was broken into by smashing the door down and the computer, switchboard and fax machine were stolen. The stolen equipment was, of necessity, immediately replaced and the owners improved the security by fitting heavy steel cages over the windows and door secured with massive bolts through the walls. Within a week it was burgled again: the new security devices being dealt with by chaining the door cage to a car and driving off! All the kit was stolen again. The insurers were now beginning to bleat and in order to satisfy them the door and frame were replaced with a steel ones which presented a completely smooth outer face. The windows were also fitted with smooth steel shutters; the idea being that if they can't get hold of it they can't remove it! Sure enough the thief returned: he didn't bother with the door or windows — he smashed his way through the roof! (For those that haven't twigged, the thief knew that each time he burgled the place the stolen equipment would be replaced — so he just kept coming back!)

So what can you do? Try the following measures:

(a) Obviously wood is out as the main

construction material. The outer leaf could be constructed from brick as previously suggested or it could be sheathed in 3mm sheet steel. This is not such a daft idea as it sounds because steel is very cheap and easily joined by stitch welding. To make the structure fireproof it must be stood off from the wood below by at least 12mm and the corners must be sealed by stitch welding to a steel angle running the height of the wall. To limit the success of the local artists weld on mesh trellises and grow any evergreen vine or ivy. After a couple of years the whole outer wall area will be invisible.

(b) The door and windows must be protected by steel shutters which are completely smooth on the outside and which fit closely to the walls. The window shutters can be top hinged and fitted with lower edge bolts which pass through tubes into the inside where nuts with 50mm square washers tacked on are run onto the threads. The thread should be at least 20mm diameter. The shutter should be built up onto a steel angle frame onto which the hinge bolts and securing bolts are welded and their actual position should not be visible from outside. Obviously the hinge bolts should be free to rotate but so should the fixing bolts. Make these by welding gussets into the corner of the angle with a pin passing through the end of the bolt and holes in the gussets. Slide the gussets onto the pin and then weld into the frame so it cannot be taken apart. The sheeting of the shutter should be at least 3mm steel and continuously welded to the frame or returned around the back of it.

(c) The door should be treated similarly but the real problem with it is the lock. All I can suggest is that decent deadlocks are built into the (preferably steel) door itself so that it is first locked and the steel shutter closed over it. The steel shutter should itself be locked by a pair of substantial bolts fixed in the same way as the rear door of a van — both connected by a twist lever which pushes and pulls the bolts vertically. The bolts themselves should be driven into holes in steel plates fixed from inside the workshop. The twist lever can be locked by the heaviest duty deadlock or deadbolt that you can find which engages with a cut-out in the mechanism in the closed position. Obviously the deadlock must be mounted on the inside of the shutter on studs welded to take it and the key passed through a hole in the shutter. The twist lever should be removable so that only a square hole is left — otherwise the local crooks will simply snap the lever off flush and really mess you up!

(d) The roof is something which most people overlook as a point of entry — including my friends! If fire is a possibility then it must be sheathed in steel or aluminium. If it is of another form of construction other than wood (such as tiles) then you could fix heavy 100mm square mesh just under the rafters. Alternatively the ceiling inside the workshop could be replaced by steel or aluminium with sheet polystyrene stuck on for insulation and decoration.

At the end of your efforts you should have a completely bland and featureless box with not a single edge or fixing sticking out which the thieves can get a chain or a jemmy behind.

120

If something does go walkies

If you are unfortunate enough to 'lose' something you could find yourself in a very difficult situation. Just take a minute to think of something you have made and then describe it, in the same way you would to the authorities, so that there would be no question that if it is found it is indeed yours. While you're at it, try to describe it so the authorities know what they are looking for in the first place! Yours will not be the only BO-BO locomotive model or reproduction Henry VIII commode ever made. The thief, if caught, may claim that he actually made it and not you.

You must mark and photograph any models or items of equipment that are at risk of being lost . Markers can be purchased very cheaply and all that you need do is to put your postcode in a few places. Place at least one mark in a position that will not involve any dismantling because the police use highlighting equipment to check all retrieved property. The presence of a postcode will enable them to identify the true owner even if you have not yet reported it missing. Photographing every item is also a helpful means of identification for the police, and specialist periodicals supporting your particular hobby may be prepared to publish both a picture and a description.

Crime will never be stopped. All the indications are that it is going to get considerably worse. No-one is immune, no matter how well protected his or her property may be, *but that should not stop people from doing their utmost to reduce the risk.*

Finally, as a means of brightening an otherwise sombre and depressing subject, I can relate a story that I read in the press some time ago that shows that occasionally the criminal doesn't get it all his own way. The story concerned a lady who owned two pet Alsatians who also acted as guard dogs. On one occasion when she was away on holiday her neighbour, who was feeding the dogs through a hole in the garden fence as a safety precaution, was concerned at the non-appearance of one of the dogs. Fearing that the dog was ill, the neighbour was waiting at the gate for the return of the owner several days later. The owner rushed into the house and was relieved to find both the dogs perfectly fit and well – *which is more than could be said for the burglar they had pinned up against a wall in the lounge!*

CHAPTER 11

Insurance matters

In the previous chapter on security I stated that most people are surprisingly lax in protecting themselves against the very real danger of being burgled. Guess what? We're no better when it comes to insurance! Consider the following list of questions:

(1) Is your workshop insured?
(2) Is it covered by your household contents, or perhaps, by your building insurance?
(3) What about the creations that you have spent up to ten years building — are they covered for their true value — are they insured at all?
(4) What if your latest invention goes berserk and destroys not only the workshop but the house as well?

The chances are that the vast majority of people have never given much thought to the subject, let alone know the answers to any of the questions. I must admit that I didn't know the answers either but, as the famous saying goes, I know a man who does!

To try to obtain answers to these and other pertinent questions I thought up every possible query that I could and approached one of the most well known

insurance companies in this country, Sun Alliance Insurance UK. As a result I am especially indebted to Sun Alliance and the Superintendent of the Household Customer Services Division, Mr K. MacGregor, who took the time to provide detailed answers to each question.

In order to give some structure to the subject I divided the questions into three areas: the buildings, the contents — tools and the contents — models. I hope that you find all of the answers that you need among them.

The buildings

Most workshops fall into one of the following categories:

(a) Purpose built or adapted brick structure.
(b) Purpose built or adapted all wood structure.
(c) Partitioned off area in an existing structure such as a garage. This is probably the most common type.
(d) The average size is probably in the order of 3m × 2m.

Q *Do any of these require a specific type of cover or an extension of the normal building policy which must already exist* on the domestic property? This relates to building loss rather than contents.

A None of the categories mentioned would require a specific type of cover or extension to the normal domestic buildings policy.

Q *Are wooden building disadvantaged as far as insurance cover is concerned specifically in relation to the probable total loss in the event of fire?*

A Buildings of non-standard construction (that is, not built of brick, stone or concrete or with a tiled roof) may represent a greater fire hazard. This is certainly the case with regard to buildings of wood construction. In respect of the whole house, where a workshop of wooden construction represents a substantial proportion of the risk, this may need to be reflected in the terms and premium applied to the policy.

Q *Most workshops will be supplied with electricity only. Some though could have large bottles of Calor type gas, oxyacetylene or flammable solvents. What effect would these have on the preparation of a premium or in the settlement of a claim? There are of course two situations to consider; the flammable substances were the primary cause of the loss, or, the flammable substances simply worsened an existing loss situation.*

A Likewise, the storage of flammable solvents and bottles of gas increases the chances of a fire or explosion occurrence. Full details should be disclosed to the insurer. As a general guideline, we recommend that, whenever possible, all such combustible materials are stored away from the house.

The contents — tools

The contents of a workshop can vary considerably. In general there will be fixed machinery such as lathes, a drilling machine, milling machine and other smaller items. In general most of these items would require partial dismantling before removal. There will also be a quantity of handtools and attachments lying loose. The value can vary considerably and could be from £1,500 to above £10,000.

Q *Would the Insurers expect the existence of this valuable equipment to be specifically declared?*

A Tools used solely for personal use and which are included within the Contents Sum Insured* are normally covered. However, where there is some business use involved or if the tools concerned are of particularly high value, details should be referred to the insurer.

Q *Would the contents be best covered by an independent policy or simply by an extension to the existing house contents insurance?*

A Cover can usually be included under the existing domestic insurance policy. Should the tools form part of the policyholder's business then a separate policy may be more appropriate. Again, the insurance company should be contacted for advice.

Q *It is not very likely that the loss of all equipment would occur as a result of a burglary as it is all rather specialised – and very heavy! Apart from small individual losses the most likely cause for a large claim would be through the total destruction of the building. Would this affect the premium?*

A Premiums are calculated on the total values at risk and we do not allow for selection of particular items against specific perils. Therefore, the premium is not affected.

---

* It is up to the insured to value the contents of a property and then obtain suitable cover to that value. Therefore, when assessing the cover required, you should allow for the value of the workshop contents.

Q *If the structure is independent of the main building would a certain minimum level of security be demanded by the Insurers?*

A This will all depend on the individual circumstances of the risk.

Q *If the owner of the structure can demonstrate that extensive security measures have been taken would this affect the premium?*

A In certain instances, a discount is given in recognition of good home security but this does depend upon the individual circumstances.

Q *Would the Insurers be in a position to advise on the most effective types of security based on experience?*

A We are happy to offer our policyholders advice on home security. Also, the local Crime Prevention Officer is a good source of information.

Q *Would an 'as new' policy be available?*

A Replacement as new cover is available.

The contents — models

I don't know if you are familiar with the type of models constructed by the modelling fraternity but the word 'model' often seems totally inadequate as a description. In some cases they are true working miniature replicas of full size steam engines. In the case of a large prototype then the model isn't so miniature; often weighing 200kg or more! These beautiful creations can represent many thousands of hours work by the builder and up to £3,000 in the cost of raw materials alone. It is these items that are most likely to be the reason for a burglary.

Q *Should each model above a certain perceived value be individually insured?*

A Each policy should be checked carefully in order to ascertain whether items need to be individually insured. Where there is any doubt, advice should be sought from the insurer.

Q *Would a 'true value' insurance policy be available?*

A Most policies will provide to replace or economically repair damaged items.

Q *Would any special security measures be required by the Insurer and would they have any effect on the premium?*

A This will depend upon the particular risk concerned.

Q *To model engineers one of the most satisfying parts of the hobby is displaying their handiwork or giving rides at public events. Ignoring matters concerning public liability, (which I believe is covered by the venue normally), what is the position regarding models in transit or stored on site in, say, an estate car or caravan?*

A Most domestic contents policies can be extended to cover models at public events and the transportation to and from these. The premiums and terms applicable may vary in accordance with each risk.

Q *In the event of a loss, (total or partial), occurring to an individual who simply carries adequate building and contents insurance as per an ordinary household, what would be the Insurers response to receiving a claim involving such a loss?*

A Each case would be looked at on its own individual merits. Generally speaking, provided the sums insured adequately reflect the value of the contents and the full rebuilding cost of the property, claims will be viewed sympathetically.

It would seem from the answers received that provided the level of cover purchased by the insured is sufficient to cover the worst event of total loss, then modellers need only to make special arrangements for very high value or near irreplaceable items in their possession. To stress the point further: it is important to realise that although the level of insurance may be sufficient to cover a particular loss, the insurance company will assess the payment on the basis of having covered the whole risk — not just the bit that was lost.

I will close the chapter with Mr. MacGregor's advice "I would stress to any policyholder who is uncertain about their cover to contact their insurance company for advice".

APPENDIX

Tables and data

One of the real problems with data conversion is that you end up with funny numbers. Imperial dimensions do not convert into metric numbers. 2 in converts into 50.8mm but 50.8 is not a metric number – 50 is. So, the following conversions are given in the form of metric numbers for use by constructors where true metric sizes are in use and converted for imperial users who are confronted by metricated sizes:

	MASS			LENGTH	
Imperial	Metric	Converted	Imperial	Metric	Converted
1 lb	0.5 kg	0.5 kg	0.5 in	10 mm	12 mm
2 lb	1 kg	0.9 kg	1 in	25 mm	25 mm
1 cwt			1.5 in	40 mm	38 mm
(112 lb)	50 kg	51 kg	2 in	50 mm	51 mm
1 ton			3 in	75 mm	76 mm
(2240 lb)	1000 kg	1016 kg	4 in	100 mm	102 mm
			5 in	125 mm	127 mm
			6 in	150 mm	152 mm
			7 in	175 mm	178 mm
			8 in	200 mm	203 mm
			9 in	225 mm	229 mm
			10 in	250 mm	254 mm
			11 in	275 mm	279 mm
			1 ft	300 mm	305 mm
			6 ft	2 m	1.8 m
			8 ft	2.5 m	2.4 m
			10 ft	3 m	3 m

USEFUL CONVERSIONS

Imperial			Metric		
1 gallon	–	4.54 ltr	1 ltr	–	0.219 gal
1 cu.ft	–	0.028 cu.m	1 cu.m	–	35.3 cu.ft
1 cu.yd	–	0.76 cu.m	1 kg	–	2.2 lb
1 lb	–	0.45 kg	1 tonne	–	0.98 ton
1 in	–	25.4 mm	1 kw	–	1.34 hp
1 hp	–	0.745 kw			

MATERIALS

Builders' sand:	Fine sand, used for mortar and rendering.
Sharp sand:	Coarse sand, used for concrete and screeds.
Aggregate:	Stones graded by size, used for concrete in the ballast.
Ballast:	75% aggregate, 25% sharp sand, used for concrete.
Pea shingle:	Fine stones, used for drainage channels.
Damp-proof membrane:	1000 grade plastic sheet.
Vapour barrier:	500 grade plastic sheet.
Damp-proof course:	115mm wide textured plastic.
Sheet insulation:	Extruded polystyrene.
Weatherboard:	Feathered edged planks.
Shiplap boarding:	Contoured or profiled planks.

MIXES

General purpose concrete	5 parts ballast, 1 part cement.
Floor screed:	5 parts sharp sand, 1 part cement.
Mortar:	5 parts builders' sand, 1 part cement.

QUANTITIES

50kg of fine concrete mix:	Produces 0.23 sq.m concrete 100mm thick or 0.023 cu.m.
1 cwt of fine concrete mix:	Produces 2.45 sq.ft concrete 4 in. thick or 0.812 cu.ft.
50kg of fine concrete mix:	Requires approx 4.25 litres of water for a stiff mix.
1 cwt of fine concrete mix:	Requires approx 7.5 pints of water for a stiff mix.

NOTE: For all normal purposes 50kg = 1 cwt

Index